BE YOUR OWN SE[LF]

To Rich,

A real pleasure to have worked with you in my first "Be Your Own Self" Ester Lord "workshop

Best wishes,

Jeremy

Dr Jerome Carson is a clinical psychologist. He holds posts at the Institute of Psychiatry, part of King's College London, and the South London and Maudsley NHS Trust. He has been running self-esteem workshops since 1996 for health and social care professionals. He has co-edited three books and written or co-authored over 100 journal articles.

BE YOUR OWN SELF-ESTEEM COACH

The *definitive guide* to boosting your self-confidence by an experienced clinical psychologist

Jerome Carson
BA(Hons), MSc, PhD, C.Psychol.

Whiting & Birch Ltd

MMVI

© Jerome Carson, 2006
All rights reserved. No part of this publication may be reproduced in any form without permission.
Published by Whiting & Birch Ltd,
London SE23 3HZ, England.
British Library Cataloguing in Publication Data.
A CIP catalogue record is available from the British Library
ISBN 1 86177 052 9 (limp)
Printed in England by Athenaeum Press

CONTENTS

Introduction --- 7

1. What is self-esteem? --- 11
2. What has influenced
   your own self-esteem development? -------------------------- 17
3. Nurturing or enhancing your own self-esteem -------------- 27
4. Maintaining your level of self-esteem ------------------------ 61
5. Concluding comments -- 79

References --- 83

Appendix One:.
Self-Esteem Quotations -- 85

Appendix Two:
Inspirational Prose and Poetry ------------------------------------- 95

Appendix Three:
Affirmations -- 101

INTRODUCTION

Most of you reading this book will not have had the chance to attend my workshops of the same title, *'Be Your Own Self-Esteem Coach.'* In writing this book, it is my intention to take you through most of the material that I cover in workshops and also to provide you with more information than it is possible to cram into a one day workshop.

Why another book on self-esteem?

There are hundreds of books and thousands of scientific articles on the topic of self-esteem. Why add another to this burgeoning literature? The fact that there are so many books shows how important the issue of self-esteem is. It also highlights the fact that the secrets of a healthy self-esteem remain elusive. Every writer on this topic probably feels that they have something unique to contribute to the topic, and in that respect I suppose I am no different.

Lizzie Gardiner once told me that *'We teach best what we most need to learn.'* Following this reasoning, I must have a personal need to better understand the topic of self-esteem and that it has an intimate connection for my own life. As someone who has been running self-esteem workshops for over a decade, I would like to think that I have learned to develop a more robust sense of self-esteem. The fact is that self-esteem is never static. Life's troubles have a habit of shaking even the hardiest amongst us.

This book is based on three main influences. First, an appreciation of the best published literature on the topic of self-esteem. Second, my experiences from trying to boost the self-esteem of hundreds of participants in my self-esteem workshops. These individuals have taught me huge lessons about the resilience of the human spirit, even amongst the most adverse of circumstances. Third, my developing understanding of the concept of self-esteem and of its role in each of our lives.

As we shall see later, the origins of our self-esteem lie in our childhoods and our upbringing. As the expression goes, *'The child is the father of the man.'* This is as true for me as it is for every reader. In the chapters that follow, we will all pause to think how our individual self-esteem has been shaped by the key influences in our own lives.

My involvement with self-esteem

It was Dr Will Davies who developed a three day programme, *'Enhancing Self-Esteem,'* and this was the first self-esteem workshop that I facilitated in 1996. From the start, I was keen to incorporate some of my own ideas about self-esteem into the programme. I expanded my doctoral thesis into staff stress to include evaluations of these self-esteem workshops. Professor Elizabeth Kuipers and Professor Dave Hemsley supervised this research. While the thesis was largely concerned with the issues of what stressed mental health professionals in their work, in it I presented some evidence to suggest that enhancing staff self-esteem could serve as a protective factor in counter-acting occupational stress.

Be Your Own Self-Esteem Coach

Why write a book called *Be Your Own Self-Esteem Coach?* As we shall see later, the issue of self-esteem is to do with the relationship you have with yourself. A young man who attended one of my workshops in Birmingham once said, *'What do we have at the end of the day? At the end of the day we have ourselves.'* Truly, at the end of day we may only have ourselves to rely on. It is therefore even more critical that we become our own best friends and have a positive view of ourselves. We need to become our own coaches. Just as a good coach will try and get the best out of her players, we too need to get the best out of ourselves. We need to better understand what motivates us, what approaches work best with ourselves, and how to reward ourselves when we achieve our goals.

In my three day workshops, I get participants to do a presentation on the third day on some topic related to their own self-esteem issues. Clearly the prospect of doing a presentation in front of a group of people puts fear into many people. One of the ways I encourage them to believe that they can do this, is by pointing out how they are the

INTRODUCTION

world authority on themselves. They have a unique perspective on their own lives, not only as they have lived them, but also as they are the only ones who know their inner worlds as well. When many people meet me socially and discover that I am a psychologist, one of the reactions that I get, is that I will be able to miraculously discover their most intimate thoughts and secrets. Sadly, as a clinician with over 25 years experience, I am totally dependent on what my clients tell me about themselves. If they don't tell me certain things, then most of the time I can't possibly know about them. You the reader, are the world expert on yourself. Hopefully some of the material in this book will help you develop some new understandings about yourself and lead to an even deeper appreciation of your uniqueness.

How to use this book?

This is not a book to be read at a single sitting. Rather take your time. Reflect, especially on any part that resonates with your own experience. Do the exercises in the book. Make a note of significant points for you, that you may especially need to work on.

The attitude of gratitude

Before getting started on this quest of becoming our own self-esteem coach, I would like to pause and pay thanks to the people that have helped me on my own quest. Over the years I have been blessed to have had the support and encouragement of numerous professional colleagues. Professor Kevin Gournay, Dr Frank Holloway and Sam Antwi-Marful have all made unique contributions to helping me progress. My publisher David Whiting believed in this project, and has moved at record pace to get this book into press. I will always be grateful to you David for this support! It has involved impossible deadlines that we both managed somehow to meet. My partner Maggie, has had to put up with many of my wild ideas. She also proof read the entire book and gave me very helpful comments to keep me on task and suggestions on how to improve the clarity of the manuscript.

In my personal life, my first and best coach was my mother, who died suddenly when I was only sixteen. Luckily, my Aunt Teresa and Uncle Frank took over some of my mother's work and had a profound influence on me over the years. One of the many things they provided me with was unconditional positive regard. This is where someone loves you, no matter what you do in your own life. I am sure that at times I may have been a great disappointment to them, yet it never stopped them loving me, even to this day. My children and grandchildren will scan this book with more than curiosity, as at times they have been my harshest critics. Expressions such as, 'Dad, I thought you were meant to be boosting my self-esteem,' show how I may not always have practiced what I preached. Many other people in my personal and professional life have believed in me at various times during my life's journey. I only hope that they have felt that I appreciated their support. In terms of my knowledge of the concept of self-esteem, I owe the greatest debt to the hundreds of workshop participants and also the hundreds of patients who have taught and continue to teach me its lessons. It is to them that this book is dedicated.

ONE

WHAT IS SELF-ESTEEM?

In our society, one might speak of an epidemic of low self-esteem ... Maybe we are overdeveloped outwardly and underdeveloped inwardly. Perhaps it is we who, for all our wealth, are living in poverty. Jon Kabat-Zinn.

When I started running self-esteem workshops, entering the keyword self-esteem into an internet search engine provided 50,736 hits. Repeating this exercise in April 2006 generated some 5,500,839 hits. The on-line bookstore Amazon.com registered some 2,685 books on the subject of self-esteem. What has always been a topic of interest has clearly mushroomed almost out of control. Whatever self-esteem is, it is clearly very popular.

There have been numerous attempts to define the nature of self-esteem. Will Davies described it as *'a realistic and positive view of oneself which has a beneficial effect on everything one does.'* The psychiatrist Philip Robson describes it thus, *'The sense of contentment and self-acceptance that results from a person's appraisal of his/her own worth, significance, attractiveness, competence and ability to satisfy his or her aspirations.'*

One of the best known writers in this area, Morris Rosenberg states that self-esteem is, *'the evaluation which the individual makes and customarily maintains with regard to him or herself: it expresses an attitude of approval or disapproval toward oneself.'* There are three main aspects:

Reflected appraisal is how I think other people see me.

Social comparison is how I compare myself with others.

Self-attribution, finally, is how I judge myself on my performance.

The Oxford Reference Dictionary put it most succinctly, defining it as a *'good opinion of oneself.'*

One of the major writers in this field, is the American psychologist Nathaniel Branden. He feels there are two elements to the definition of self-esteem. These are:

1. Confidence in our ability to think and cope with the basic challenges of life or self-efficacy (essentially the ability to do or perform).

2. Confidence in our right to be happy, the feeling of being worthy, deserving, entitled to assert our needs and wants and to enjoy the fruits of our efforts (self-respect).

Christopher Mruk, talks in similar terms of competence and worthiness.

I would concur with both these authors in stating that **self-esteem comprises two elements, self-worth and personal competence.** So to tackle the problem of low self-esteem, we need to tackle both the issue of low self-worth and also possible low competence. These two dimensions can be independent. So it may be possible to have a low level of life skills, yet believe that one has very high self-worth. Conversely, it can be possible to have very high levels of competence in some domains of your life, but yet feel worthless. To develop our sense of self-esteem we need to work on self-worth and also personal competence.

This is a theme that I will keep coming back to throughout the book, however before doing so, I want to add a bit more flesh onto the self-esteem model.

While stating that there were two key elements of self-esteem, Branden stated that these were held up by six pillars. These were:

- *living consciously,*
- *self-acceptance,*
- *self-responsibility,*
- *self-assertiveness,*
- *living purposefully and*
- *personal integrity.*

Susan Graham has translated these as,

- *thinking about what I am doing,*
- *I am what I am,*
- *I am in charge of me,*

WHAT IS SELF-ESTEEM?

- *what I think matters,*
- *aiming for what I want and*
- *I believe this and that's OK or rules I live by.*

In this country Titus Alexander argues that there are nine elements to self-esteem. These are:

- *unconditional self-acceptance,*
- *sense of capability,*
- *sense of purpose,*
- *appropriate assertiveness,*
- *experience of flow and fulfilment,*
- *sense of responsibility and accountability,*
- *sense of safety and security,*
- *sense of belonging and*
- *sense of integrity.*

There is clearly some overlap in Branden and Alexanders' views.

Why should we concern ourselves about self-esteem?

Well, why *should* we concern ourselves about self-esteem in the first place. Is it really that important?

In the original Association of Psychological Therapies Enhancing Self-Esteem programme Will Davies made two main points.

For the first, he borrowed a metaphor from the American motivational speaker and author, Jack Canfield. This is the metaphor of the poker chips. A person gambling, who has 100 chips, is more likely to take risks, than the person with only five chips. So the person with high self-esteem is more likely to take risks in the game we call life, than the person with low self-esteem. One of my male patients recently asked a woman to go out with him. This was the first person he asked in my five years of working with him. She turned him down. It is my prediction that he will wait another five years before he asks anyone else!

Will's second analogy was derived from the work of the psychiatrist Aaron Beck, the father of cognitive behaviour therapy (CBT). Beck argues that patients with depression and anxiety see the world in particular ways. The depressed patient has a negative view of themselves, their world and their future. This is the so-called cognitive triad. The anxious patient on the other hand has a view of themselves as incompetent, of others as being unsupportive and of the world as being an unpredictable and threatening place. Will argues that if we can change the negative view of the depressed patient or the incompetent view of the anxious patient, we might be able to tackle the destructiveness of their thinking styles.

Low self-esteem creates problems almost the same as those of depression. However, it is worth thinking a moment about the experience of those with bipolar disorder (these are people who can alternate between spells of depression and mania). When they are high they can have grandiosely high levels of self-esteem. High self-esteem may not therefore always be desirable. Branden argues that we need to develop *healthy* self-esteem. He characterises people with healthy self-esteem as having the following qualities:

- They have a face, manner, way of talking and moving that project the pleasure one takes in being alive.

- They have an ease in talking of accomplishments or shortcomings with directness and honesty, as they are in friendly relationship to facts.

- They have a comfort in giving and receiving compliments, expressions of affection, appreciation and the like.

- They are open to criticism and comfortable about acknowledging mistakes because their self-esteem is not tied to an image of perfection.

- Their words or movements tend to have a quality of ease and spontaneity since they are not at war with themselves.

- They have a harmony between what they say and do and how they look, sound and move.

- They have an attitude of openness to and curiosity about new ideas, new experiences and new possibilities of life.

- Feelings of anxiety or insecurity if they present themselves, will be less likely to intimidate or overwhelm them, since accepting these feelings, managing them and rising above them rarely feels impossibly different.

- They have an ability to enjoy the humourous aspects of life in themselves and others.

- They are flexible in responding to situations and challenges, are moved by a spirit of inventiveness and even playfulness, since they trust their minds and do not see life as doom or defeat.

- They have an ability to preserve a quality of harmony and dignity under conditions of stress.

How many of these attributes could you tick off for yourself? I suspect that most of us could all make some improvements in many of these areas. How do we accept gifts and compliments for instance?

A final issue in introducing the concept of self-esteem, is to ask what would a good self-esteem programme look like? *Would I recognise one if I saw one?* Christopher Mruk argues that there are four elements to a good self-esteem programme. These are:

1. *It should provide an understanding of the concept of self-esteem.*

2. *It should develop a better personal awareness of the self-esteem of participants.*

3. *It should nurture or enhance the self-esteem of participants.*

4. *It should help participants know how to maintain their levels of self-esteem after the programme has ended.*

If I have done a good job in this introductory chapter, you should have developed a better awareness of the concept of self-esteem. In a nutshell, that **self-esteem is comprised of self-worth and personal competence**. If you can remember these two simple facts, then we can start looking at how other aspects of self-esteem can slot in.

One of the things that always impresses me when I conduct workshops on self-esteem, is what M.Scott Peck refers to as *'the routine heroism of human beings.'* Many so-called ordinary people have often achieved extraordinary things in their lives, and yet do not see them as such. For many people, when confronted with multiple trauma earlier in their lives, just to be alive is a huge achievement.

Finally, I want to end this first chapter by leaving you with a metaphor. Debbie Hazelton, talks about the metaphor of the dipper and the bucket (dipper is an American word for ladle). Imagine for a moment that you have a bucket at your feet. The level of water in this bucket, represents your current level of self-esteem. She goes on

BE YOUR OWN SELF-ESTEEM COACH

The amount of self-esteem in our bucket determines how we feel about ourselves and others ... Your bucket can be filled by a lot of things ... The interplay of the dipper and the bucket is the story of our lives, and everyone has both. The mystery of the dipper and the bucket is this. The only way we can fill our own bucket is to fill someone else's bucket.

This is an interesting metaphor that I will come back to later. Of course it is possible that all of us may have different buckets, eg. a work bucket and a personal bucket. It is also the case that we might have a lid on our bucket, that stops people filling it for us. As one of my patient's also reminded me, some of us may have holes in our buckets! There are also people who spend their entire lives filling up other people's buckets, but who pay no attention to their own. I suppose it all goes to show how even an apparently simple metaphor can actually be quite complex when we begin to look at the intricacies of life.

What you keep to yourself you lose, what you give away you keep forever. Axel Munthe

TWO

WHAT HAS INFLUENCED YOUR OWN SELF-ESTEEM DEVELOPMENT?

What lies behind us and what lies before us are tiny matters compared to what lies within us. Ralph Waldo Emerson.

In the last chapter I suggested that the two key issues in enhancing self-esteem are to increase your sense of self-worth and develop your level of personal competence. Yet what are the factors that determine our level of self-esteem as adults? Why is it that some of us have a high level of self-esteem and others a low level? The origins of each of our levels of self-esteem clearly lies in our upbringing and in our life experiences, along with our interpretation of these experiences.

Our first teachers in life are our parents. The nature of our relationship with our parents is one of the first major influences on us. If we are fortunate to have parents who have encouraged us in our childhood, and to have provided us with a stable upbringing, then we are more likely to grow up to be well-adjusted. Two very important factors here are whether our parents have provided us with unconditional love and time. The concept of unconditional love was an issue I highlighted in the Introduction. We have such an experience when we feel loved by our parents, no matter what our actions. So even if we transgress in life, our parents may be upset, but it does not stop them loving us. In the clinical work I have done with hundreds of patients with mental health problems, this is one of the key factors missing in their lives. Jack Canfield in his cassette *Self-Esteem and Peak Performance*, gives the example of the child who scores 99% in an exam. The father on hearing this result says to the child, '*What happened to the other one per cent?*' In terms of us all being our own self-esteem coaches, we need to ask, **did we feel unconditionally loved by our own parents, or did we feel that no matter what we did we were never fully accepted or loved?**

The second issue I mentioned above was that of time. **Did you feel that your parents made time for you,** or did you feel excluded? Did your parents attend parents' evenings at school? Did they ever go to your school plays or sports days? Anthony Parsons asks the interesting question, *'Was anyone ever heard to say on their deathbed, I wish I'd spent more time at work?'* Of course as a parent yourself, you may have had a boss who prevented your taking time off work to attend school functions. You may have had to work long hours to keep the family afloat and to pay for the two family holidays each year that the family had come to expect. If there can be a good side to unemployment or being unable to work through ill health, it is that the parent or grandparent can offer their child those two most precious of commodities, time and unconditional love. For many years I worked with a remarkable man, who was physically disabled. He was also frightened of leaving his house. Consequently he was dependent on people coming around to his house to see him. Prior to becoming disabled he had been a workaholic. His family saw very little of him. After he became disabled, his role within the family changed completely. For the first time he was able to provide his children and grandchildren with all the time and unconditional love they needed. These attributes will have enhanced the lives of his family immensely and will have helped develop each of their senses of self-esteem. These are gifts he has left them with.

For some of us, our parents may have had problems in their relationships with us. Almost always this relates to problems they had with their own parents. In a few rare cases, our parents may for some reason have actively disliked us. This may seem hard to believe. I recently assessed a young woman who told me, *'I hate my parents!'* She clearly felt this way, as she perceived that her parents hated her. The American self-help writer Dave Pelzer, in a series of best sellers, tells the story of how his mother physically and emotionally abused him during his childhood in California. He was one of three boys, but for some inexplicable reason, his mother persistently and savagely abused him alone. If you have ever read the account of his childhood, it makes horrific reading. Sadly, I have to tell you that I have come across even worse accounts in my own clinical practice! Having an abusive parent is going to affect our sense of self-esteem. In such circumstances, siblings may be important in helping you cope. Additionally, relatives may provide extra nurturing, which may go some way towards compensating for the bad experiences at home.

I mentioned my own experience in the Introduction of losing my mother at the age of sixteen. I was the eldest of five children. My youngest brother was only nine when Mum died. A year after my mother died, my father remarried. While my stepmother did her best to cope with five children, who weren't her own, it was clearly impossible for her to replace our mother. My mother's youngest sister Teresa stepped in and offered to adopt the five of us children. She did in fact have six children of her own! While my father would not agree to this, he did at least allow us to spend our summer holidays with our aunt, uncle and cousins in Ireland. So for the entire school holidays we would all go to Ireland. We all felt unconditionally loved by our aunt and uncle and this was a huge asset in each of our subsequent personal developments. I have no doubt that this was a major factor in the genesis of my own self-esteem. **So in understanding yourself, you should ask the question, did any of your aunts, uncles or siblings play a role in helping you feel better about yourself?**

Of course another major influence on all of us is the educational system. This is so beloved by all education ministers, that they all feel a need to change it in some way to improve it! Teachers have a pivotal role in determining how each of us interfaces with the educational system. For some children, going to school may actually provide some respite from an unhappy home life. While many of us have happy memories of school, for others it can be traumatic and can adversely affect their levels of self-esteem. One young man attending one of my workshops told the story of how his literacy problems affected his schooling. He was later diagnosed as having dyslexia, which accounts for the problems he had with reading and spelling at school. One of his teachers had told him, *'Listen, why don't you do us all a favour, and leave school!'* It was only much later in life that his wife encouraged him to seek help for his literacy problems. He decided to attend an evening class. At the first session the teacher announced that she was going to give the class a spelling test. She went on, *'The first word is 'anonymous,' the next word is 'abysmal,"* and so it went on for another 48 words. At the end of the test, the students were asked to hand their sheets to the person next to them to be marked. The client scored 5/50, whereas the chap whose spellings he had marked scored 45/50. When they exchanged spelling sheets the partner said, *'Don't worry, between us we got them all right!'* Each of us can no doubt remember some teachers who have had a positive effect on us and some who were a negative influence. We haven't all had inspirational teachers like the English teacher portrayed by Robin Williams in the film, *Dead Poet's Society.*

Another major influence from our childhoods in affecting our level of self-esteem, is the relationship we have with our peers. Clearly not all our friends will have had the benefit of having attended classes on 'Boosting your friend's self-esteem.' In the rough and tumble of life, peers are capable of giving us both a physical and emotional battering. Some individuals bear the long term scars of bullying at school, which last long into adulthood. School reunions offer the possibility of encounters between the bullies and the bullied. When televised, this provides excruciating television. Children are of course savage exposers of difference and will pick on others who are physically different to themselves. One psychologist in one of my workshops talked about being victimised by other children, as she was much taller than them.

The sum of these childhood and adolescent experiences contributes to the sense of self-esteem that each of us is left with. Then there are the effects of life itself. Psychologists talk a lot about life events. These are the major things that happen to us all in life. Issues such as the death of a parent, divorce, unemployment, major illnesses etc. These all exert an effect on us as individuals. Life is full of ups and downs, or as Kahlil Gibran says, 'Joy and Sorrow.'

One of the most helpful ways of looking at the effects that life has on each of us, is through drawing **a graph of life satisfaction**. This is when you try and represent the course of your entire life thus far. To do this, it is probably better to take a large sheet of paper and a marker pen. Start by drawing two lines. One at the left side of the page going up (the Y axis), which should have high and low satisfaction at the top and the bottom of the page. The line along the bottom (the x axis), should start the year you were born, and end with the present year. Along the x axis it is sometimes helpful to begin by writing some of the key dates in your own life. Mine would start in 1957, the year I was born. Some significant dates for me are 1969, the date my family left Ireland, 1973, the year my mother died, 1976-79, the years I was at University, 1981-84, when I did my clinical training, 1983, when I got married, also that year my first son was born. Once you have listed the key events, the task is to try and draw a single line which reflects the ups and downs of your life. No one's life is ever a flat line! **If you have never done this task before, then stop reading now, find some paper and give it a go!**

Task: Draw a graph of your life satisfaction.

The graph of life satisfaction enables us to see how the pattern of our lives has gone. What have been the major ups and downs for each of us? Often the birth of our children represent highs, and bereavements lows. Which way does your graph appear to be heading? In a group format, I often get participants to present their individual graphs to the group. This is an exceptionally emotionally demanding task, as it confronts each of us with the major events of each of our lives. In the following chapter, I will show you how we can convert this task from a self-awareness exercise into a self-esteem enhancing exercise.

To return to our mathematical sum analogy, the sum of all our relationships and the sum of all your life experiences will all have an effect on your self-esteem. The other remaining factor that I haven't fully emphasised much yet, is your personal interpretation of what happens to us in life. It is not so much the events or people in our lives that affect us, but how we interpret these events. Two individuals can experience the same event, yet interpret it in entirely different ways. For example two teenagers fail the same exam. One is devastated and thinks, 'My academic career is over!' The other thinks, 'Well that wasn't to be. I now know that I ought to pursue a career in …' The same event, but two differing interpretations, which will affect how each individual handles this setback. We will come back to the issue of personal interpretation in the next two chapters. So how does all of this affect your level of self-esteem? How indeed do we measure your level of self-esteem?

Going back to the bucket metaphor in Chapter 1, each of us has a sense of how full or empty our own bucket of self-esteem might be at a particular moment. This gives us a subjective but not very quantifiable method for estimating your self-esteem. An alternative method of estimating your sense of self-esteem would be to complete a self-esteem questionnaire. Magazines are often full of such brief self-tests on a whole range of personality attributes, not just self-esteem. Most of these measures are devised by journalists or experts to accompany an article on a specific topic. In the vast majority of cases, these measures have no scientific credibility at all. To meet the criteria for scientific credibility, questionnaires need to fulfil certain specifications. First, items selected for inclusion in any questionnaire have to be carefully chosen and worded. Second, the questionnaire has to have good reliability and validity. Reliability refers to the accuracy of any measure. We all know that thermometers measure temperature. However different types of thermometer may not all be as reliable. We would need to test them all to see which provided the best estimates of body temperature. The reliability of questionnaires is assessed in slightly different ways, which I won't bore you with here, but which look at issues such as test-retest reliability. So if I gave you a self-esteem questionnaire today, and again tomorrow, I would expect you to obtain very similar results. Similarly, the items should all relate to each other, if they are all measuring the same phenomenon. The other important psychometric issue is validity. Broadly speaking, this means, does a questionnaire measure what it is supposed to be measuring? This can also be measured in a variety of ways. To just pick one of these. If our self-esteem questionnaire has good correlational validity, then scores on it should relate better to other self-esteem questionnaires, than to unrelated measures. Third, we need to consider issues such as the utility of the questionnaire. Is it short, is it easy to score and interpret? Has the questionnaire been given to lots of other people, so we know what the average score should be and what would constitute a good or a bad score?

This may seem an incredibly long preamble to having you complete a very brief questionnaire. You're right! If you are still with me, read on! The questionnaire we are going to complete to assess your current level of self-esteem is the Rosenberg Self-Esteem Questionnaire. While there are scores of self-esteem questionnaires on the market, the Rosenberg Scale is the most widely used in the world literature. It meets all the criteria that I outlined above. At this point you may want to get a piece of paper and mark it with the numbers 1 to 10, to save you writing directly into your book. Here we go.

WHAT HAS INFLUENCED YOUR OWN SELF-ESTEEM DEVELOPMENT?

The Rosenberg Self-Esteem Questionnaire

Instructions for completion.
Here are a list of statements dealing with general feelings about yourself. If you strongly agree with the statement circle SA. If you agree circle A. If you disagree, circle D and if you strongly disagree with the statement circle SD. Please answer ALL the items:

	1 strongly agree	2 agree	3 disagree	4 strongly disagree
1. On the whole I am satisfied with myself.	SA	A	D	SD
2. At times I think I am no good at all.	SA	A	D	SD
3. I feel that I have a number of good qualities.	SA	A	D	SD
4. I am able to do things as well as most other people.	SA	A	D	SD
5. I feel I do not have much to be proud of.	SA	A	D	SD
6. I certainly feel useless at times.	SA	A	D	SD
7. I feel that I am a person of worth, at least on an equal plane with others.	SA	A	D	SD
8. I wish I could have more respect for myself.	SA	A	D	SD
9. All in all, I am inclined to think that I am a failure.	SA	A	D	SD
10. I take a positive attitude towards myself.	SA	A	D	SD

To score the Rosenberg Scale, first add up your scores for items 1, 3, 4, 7 and 10. This gives you a score for **A**.

Next, for items 2, 5, 6, 8 and 9 you need to reverse the score you circled. This means that if you scored 1 this becomes a 4, 2 becomes a 3, 3 becomes a 2 and 4 becomes a 1. This gives you a score for **B**.

Add the scores for **A** and **B** together. This gives you your self-esteem score. What does your score mean?

The clinical psychologist Dr Bob Wycherley in his 'Living Skills' pack has provided a very helpful table to aid interpretation of your Rosenberg score.

10-13: You see yourself very positively as a competent and valuable person. You like and respect yourself, are proud of your achievements, and feel that others approve of you and respect you.

14-16: You generally have a positive view of yourself. You feel you are as competent as others and that they view you as acceptable and worthwhile.

17-20: You have an average fairly balanced view of yourself as having both good and bad points. You feel you can usually hold your own in comparison with others and that other people see you as neither better nor worse than they are.

21-25: You tend to be somewhat negative and self-critical. You don't see yourself as being as competent as others and feel they do not respect you very much.

Above 25: You generally see yourself very negatively, as less valuable and competent than others. You tend to dislike yourself, put yourself down and feel that others look down on you.

The average score for men on this questionnaire is 14.99 and for women 15.48. For people attending my self-esteem workshops, the average score is much higher at 20.31.

The score you have just obtained is how you feel at this point in time. You may be disappointed at how high your score was. It may have been over 25 (the maximum possible is 40). Alternatively, you may have a score in the top category of 10-13, showing you have very high self-esteem at the moment. Whatever your score, it is important to remember that self-esteem scores can go up and down, depending on your circumstances when you complete the form. However at least you know now, the true level of self-esteem in your bucket at this point in time!

While I have largely concentrated on developmental aspects of self-esteem in this chapter, this is not to downplay the significance of more contemporaneous events and relationships. Clearly your current level of self-esteem can be affected by your present relationships with partners, friends and colleagues. I remember one woman who attended one of my workshops telling us that as she

WHAT HAS INFLUENCED YOUR OWN SELF-ESTEEM DEVELOPMENT?

would be dozing off to sleep at night, her husband used to whisper things into her ear, such as 'why don't you just turn over and die?' or 'You're useless.' When she was on holiday with her daughters she came to the realisation that she would be better off without a husband like this. She decided to leave him. She never looked back!

Summary

In this chapter I have asked you to think about the factors from your childhood and upbringing which may have affected your self-esteem. The graph of life satisfaction will have highlighted the major events in your life and the pattern you life has taken. We have finished the chapter by completing the **Rosenberg Self-Esteem Questionnaire** which has let us see the current level of your self-esteem. This has hopefully helped us complete the second key component of Mruks' ideal self-esteem programme and that **you have now developed a better awareness of your own self-esteem.**

> *You cannot teach people anything. You can only help them discover it within themselves.* Galileo.

THREE

NURTURING OR ENHANCING YOUR OWN SELF-ESTEEM

Life asks of every individual a contribution and it is up to that individual to discover what it should be. Viktor Frankl.

Having looked at the origins of our self-esteem and considered what factors may have influenced it, we now turn to the more practical aspects of developing your sense of self-worth and improving your sense of personal competence. In this chapter I consider a number of ways of doing both and hopefully nurturing and enhancing your self-esteem in the process.

1. Valuing your personal achievements

First, let's go back to the idea of the graph of life satisfaction, that I introduced you to in the last chapter. To get some sense of your own unique life achievements, we need to divide your life into thirds. This is easy if you are 30 years old. Consider the period 0-10 as one third, 11 to 20 as the second period and 21 to 30 as the last third. What are the three achievements that you are most proud of for each period? For the first period, people pick things like, 'I learned to ride a bike' or 'I learned to swim.' In the second period, it may be things like passing your driving test, or your 11 plus exam (this may still be the first third for some of us). You should end up with a total of nine achievements. *Of these, which three are you most proud of?* When asked what the main achievements are over an entire life span, having a family of your own often features.

Task: What are you proudest achievements?

First third of my life: 1.

2.

3.

Second third of my life: 1.

2.

3.

Last third of my life: 1.

2.

3.

NURTURING OR ENHANCING YOUR OWN SELF-ESTEEM

Overall if I was asked to list the three achievements that I was most proud of over my entire life span, they would be:

1.

2.

3.

The importance of this exercise is that it often reminds us that we have achieved a lot in our past, when we start looking back. Jack Canfield suggests listing three achievements that you will have in the next five years. This is an addition to the original technique, designed to try and shape some of your future achievements. Whatever our life histories, we have all achieved much more in life than we often realise.

2. Personal resilience and self-esteem

I am increasingly impressed in my clinical practice by the resilience displayed by many of my patients. I worked with one woman from Africa, whose husband, son, two daughters and mother were all murdered by persons unknown. She escaped to Britain with her sole remaining daughter. How on earth does someone like that survive? Equally, there were many people who survived the Nazi concentration camps, including the psychiatrist, Dr Viktor Frankl, who went on to write, '**Man's Search for Meaning**,' about his experiences. The American Psychological Association (APA), has a very helpful on-line guide called, '**The Road to Resilience**.' This guide defines resilience as, *'the process of adapting well in the face of adversity…it means bouncing back from difficult experiences.'* When you reflect back on your own life, can you think of how resilient you were in the face of a particular difficulty? This could be how you dealt with the break-up of a relationship, illness of your partner, unemployment etc. Even though these may have been great setbacks at the time, you managed to bounce back!

Task: Write down an experience where you feel you displayed resilience?

The APA guide says that there are five key factors which determine our resilience. If we have caring and supportive relationships, these can help. Making realistic plans that don't overstretch us, can also help. Having a positive view of yourself and your strengths and abilities (Both things we will come to again later in this chapter). Having good communication and problem solving skills can be a further asset. Finally, the APA state that if we have the capacity to manage strong feelings and impulses without seeming overwhelmed by them, this can help as well.

One of the projects that was developed in America following the events of September 11th was the '**Reach in, Reach Out Project.**' This aimed to try and strengthen the resilience of many Americans in the face of this enormous tragedy. Like the APA, they also came up with five factors that they felt were important in building resilience. These were:

NURTURING OR ENHANCING YOUR OWN SELF-ESTEEM

1. **Healthy coping.** You need to pay attention to your physical, emotional, mental and spiritual needs to be healthy, calm, self-aware and creative in meeting challenges.

2. They stress the importance of **self-knowledge.** This they say is knowing and accepting your self as you are, and being able to identify your strengths and weaknesses.

3. They feel it is important to have a **sense of personal meaning and perspective.** You need to be able to identify what are the important elements and values in your own life.

4. **Optimism** is their fourth factor. This they say is the ability to believe that there is a solution to even the most stressful life events.

5. Finally, they also stress the importance of **strong relationships.**

Many of these factors offer us clues as to how you can build up your personal resilience. The APA suggest 10 ways of doing this:

1. Try and make more connections in your personal and community support networks. Many organisations are often looking for volunteers to help out eg. in becoming a school governor or in joining the board of a charitable organisation.

2. Avoid seeing crises as insurmountable problems. Remember the things you have successfully coped with in the past. There is a solution to the problem that is confronting you, you may just not have seen it yet.

3. Accept that change is part of living. We are all creatures of habit and like to settle into familiar and predictable routines. Anyone who has worked in the health and education sectors will know that change is a fact of life. You may as well accept the inevitability of change.

4. Move towards your goals even if it is by a very small step at a time. I have failed my black belt in Karate three times. I am slowly starting towards preparing for a fourth attempt later this year.

5. Take decisive action. At times in life we have no alternative but to

have to act decisively, rather than dither. Taking decisive action will prove to you that you have a greater degree of personal control than you believed.

6. Look for opportunities for self-discovery. Even setbacks offer you the chance to look at your situation differently. Every cloud can in fact have a silver lining!

7. Nurture a positive view of yourself. Positivity is a theme I will be coming back to later in this chapter.

8. Keep things in perspective. 'One swallow doesn't make a summer.' In the grand scheme of things how big is your particular problem? Would it make the front page of the local free newspaper?

9. Maintain a hopeful outlook. Life is full of ups and downs. While you may be down at the moment, things may take a turn for the better when you least expect them to.

10. Take care of yourself. Often when we hit difficulties, you may eat and drink too much. You need to ensure that when the pressure is on, that you create some space to look after your own personal needs.

The APA Guide concludes, that **you need to use the strategies that will work best for you!**

3. Self-image, self-belief and self-esteem

In my self-esteem workshops, I have participants do three paper and pencil exercises to consider their self-image and self-belief. In turn we see how these relate to their self-esteem. One of the first exercises I do is the Twenty Statements Test. This offers you a chance to think of how you describe yourself.

Task: To do the Twenty Statements Test complete the phrases as follows:

I am ………………………………………………………
I am………………………………………………………
I am………………………………………………………
I am………………………………………………………
I am………………………………………………………
I am……………………………………………………..
I am……………………………………………………..
I am……………………………………………………..
I am……………………………………………………..
I am……………………………………………………..
I am……………………………………………………
I am……………………………………………………
I am…………………………………………………..
I am…………………………………………………..
I am…………………………………………………
I am…………………………………………………
I am…………………………………………………
I am…………………………………………………
I am…………………………………………………
I am…………………………………………………

Most people find it hard to come up with 20 statements. This is an open or projective test. There are no right or wrong answers. You have to come up with the statements that apply to you. As there are no right or wrong answers, it is more of an exploratory or discussion tool. Rees and Nicholson believe that responses fall into five major categories.

1. Skills, abilities and attainments. These are cognitive, social, technical, organisational or achieving.

2. Interests, needs and motives. These are need for achievement, power, affiliation, growth, arts, work, orientation, physical and active.

3. Character style. These are outgoing, conceptual, confident, impulsive, open to experience, caring, well-being, self-appreciation, emotional, reliable and introspective.

4. Values and beliefs. These are religious, political, ethical and psychological.

5. Others. Miscellaneous and expectations.

Which of these categories did your responses mainly fall into?

A second exercise I use in workshops is one I have adapted from Lynda Field's book, *The Self-Esteem Workbook*. Here she provides a long list of adjectives that could be used to describe you. From her list, you select the ones that most and least apply to you. You then choose six adjectives that are your best descriptors. From these you select the one that is the most important. This she says is your core-belief. What does it reveal about you? Does it criticise or support you? Does it support low or high self-esteem? According to Lynda Field, having a positive self-belief leads to positive expectations, which in turn leads to decisive behaviour and increased self-esteem.

The third task I use in workshops is taken from Mark Warner's book, *The Complete Idiot's Guide to Enhancing Self-Esteem*. This is an exercise with six parts.

1. If your best friend were asked to say what are your three greatest gifts, talents or abilities, what would they say?

2. What do you think are your three greatest talents or abilities?

3. What is one major life experience that had a profound effect on your life? What life treasure did it leave you with?

4. What are three things you want others to say about you?

5. What has been your greatest accomplishment?

6. What project are you currently undertaking that elicits excitement from you?

How you see yourself affects your self-esteem. If you see yourself positively, then you are more likely to have high self-esteem. Conversely, if you have a negative self-image, then you are more likely to have low self-esteem.

4. Optimism and self-esteem.

A pessimist sees the difficulty in every opportunity: an optimist sees the opportunity in every difficulty. Winston Churchill

Put simply, optimists are people who expect good things to happen to them. Pessimists are people who expect bad things to come their way. Like self-esteem itself, optimism has its origins in our backgrounds and may even be in our genetic make-up. Children who grow up in predictable and secure backgrounds with stable attachment figures are more likely to be optimists later in life, than children from disruptive backgrounds. **Which of these would you say characterises your own background?**

Optimism is even implicated in a range of physical conditions. Levels of optimism in the first trimester of pregnancy predict anxiety in the third. Optimism predicts post-natal depression. Optimism is a strong predictor of the response to a diagnosis of cancer. Optimists see the burden of caring as less onerous. It would also appear that optimists use different types of coping strategies than pessimists. They tend to seek out information more, use active coping and planning, try to positively reframe situations, use humour and accept the situation more than pessimists. Optimists tend to see the best in bad situations and try to learn something from them.

Karen Millard argues that there are a number of good reasons why you should be an optimist. Optimism convinces us that our actions matter. It helps us feel that we are 'the captains of our ships.' Optimists tend to persevere, they are more patient, they look for a more meaningful explanation, they are healthier, more resilient, more proactive and feel better. They even believe they can move mountains! But how do you know if you are an optimist or a pessimist? Martin Seligman in his book *Learned Optimism* provides a 48 item questionnaire that measures optimism. However, I have chosen to share with you the Life Orientation Test-Revised, which only has 10 items and is considerably easier to interpret and score.

The Life Orientation Test-Revised

Please be as honest and accurate as you can throughout. Try not to let your response to one statement influence your response to other statements. There are no correct or incorrect answers. Answer according to your own feelings, rather than how you think most people would answer. Circle a number next to each statement.

5 = I agree a lot
4 = I agree a little
3 = I neither agree or disagree
2 = I disagree a little
1 = I disagree a lot

1. In uncertain times, I usually expect the best	5	4	3	2	1
2. It's easy for me to relax	5	4	3	2	1
3. If something can go wrong for me it will	5	4	3	2	1
4. I'm always optimistic about my future	5	4	3	2	1
5. I enjoy my friends a lot	5	4	3	2	1
6. It's important for me to keep busy	5	4	3	2	1
7. I hardly ever expect things to go my way	5	4	3	2	1
8. I don't get upset too easily	5	4	3	2	1
9. I rarely count on good things happening to me	5	4	3	2	1
10. Overall, I expect more good things to happen to me than bad	5	4	3	2	1

Of the 10 items on this scale, four are fillers. That is they don't count towards the total score. These are items 2, 5, 6 and 8. Of the remainder, the OPTIMISM items are items 1, 4 and 10. To get your optimism score, you add up your scores for these items. The minimum score is 3, the maximum is 15. The PESSIMISM items are items, 3, 7 and 9. Again the minimum score is 3 and the maximum is 15. What is your Optimism score? What is your Pessimism score? The bigger the difference in terms of Optimism, ie. a maximum of 12, then the more optimistic you are. This scale can also be scored by reversing the Pessimism items so 5 becomes 1, 4 = 2, 3 = 3, 2 = 4 and 1 = 5. This would then leave you with one total score. The Life Orientation Test was devised to assess individual differences in generalised optimism versus pessimism. (See Scheier, M. Carver, C. and Bridges, M. 1994, 'Distinguishing optimism from neuroticism and trait anxiety, self-mastery and self-esteem: A re-evaluation of the Life Orientation Test. Journal of Personality and Social Psychology, 67, 1063-1078 *or on-line,* http://www.psy.miami.edu/faculty/ccarver/sclLOT-R.html.

The Optimism items were 'In uncertain times I usually expect the best,' 'I'm always optimistic about my future' and 'Overall, I expect more good things to happen to me than bad.' There is increasing research evidence that optimists are happier, wealthier and healthier than pessimists. While the world would be a pretty boring place if we were all optimists and pessimists had been banished, by the same token, **optimism clearly has many more benefits to commend it to us than pessimism.**

5. Cognitive Behaviour Therapy.

The National Institute for Clinical Effectiveness (NICE) is often in the news for its decisions on which drugs doctors should prescribe for which medical conditions. What is often not so well known, is that it also expresses opinions on which psychological treatments may be best for specific mental disorders. In this era of evidence based psychiatry, cognitive behaviour therapy (CBT for short) is King. It has been the most recommended of all the psychological therapies. Melanie Fennel in her book *Overcoming Low Self-Esteem*, has written one of the best accounts of how to apply CBT to problems of low self-esteem. Melanie highlights a number of key questions that can help you find alternatives to any self-critical thoughts you may have. For instance, imagine the situation where your partner has left you and ended your two year relationship. You are so upset by this, that you begin to believe that you may never find happiness again. Melanie would stop you at that point and try and guide you through a series of structured questions.

1. **What is the evidence?**
   Are you confusing a thought with a fact? What is the evidence in favour of the thought that you will never have a new relationship? What is the evidence against this thought?

2. **What alternative perspectives are there?**
   Are you assuming that your perspective is the only one possible? What evidence do you have to support an alternative perspective?

3. **What is the effect of thinking the way I do about myself?**
   Do these self-critical thoughts actually help you? Are they getting in the way of you moving on? What perspective might be more helpful to you?

4. **What are the biases in your thinking about yourself?**
   Do you show any of the following thinking distortions? Are you jumping to conclusions? Are you using double standards? Are you thinking in all or nothing terms? Are you concentrating on your weaknesses and forgetting your strengths? Are you condemning yourself on the basis of a single event? Are you blaming yourself for things which are not really your fault? Are you expecting yourself to be perfect?

5. **What can you do?**
   How do you put a new kinder perspective into practice? Is there anything you need to do to change the situation? Even if not, what can you do to change your own thinking about it in future? How can you experiment with acting in a less self-defeating way?

At times all of us in life are prone to misinterpret situations and events and we all need some CBT. **Excessively negative thinking is clearly the bedfellow of low self-esteem.**

6. Inspirational figures and role models

If you think again about your own life and upbringing as you were doing in Chapter 2, **what individuals most enhanced your own self-esteem**? It may have been one of your parents, a sibling, a grandparent, a friend, a teacher, a colleague. In more recent years, it may be your partner. Different individuals will have had an influence on each of our lives. Who was the key person, or persons, who most influenced your self-esteem in a positive way? Who really believed in you and nurtured you? In one of my workshops, one participant, let's call him Bob, told the story of while on a boat, he had walked out onto the deck. He noticed a man's hands over the side of the boat. Bob calmly spoke to this man and persuaded him not to let go. He managed to persuade the man to come back onto the boat and not take his life. This was the individual whom Bob felt had profoundly affected his self-esteem, even though theirs had been an entirely brief and chance encounter. Their meeting had given Bob a sense of personal agency. That he could change things in life for the better. The people that each of us may have chosen may not have had such an instantaneous dramatic effect on our lives, as the above example, but their influence has become apparent over time. If the person you have chosen is still alive, have you ever told them how much they meant to you? If you haven't already done so, now may be a good time to write them a note of gratitude. Thinking of someone who has positively influenced your own self-esteem connects us with attributes in ourselves that these individuals may have nurtured in us. While some of these people may no longer be around, their positive influence lives on through us.

Are there any public figures that you admire? Some of these people may serve to inspire you. Who are the people that you most admire in the public domain? Reading their accounts of their own struggles with adversity, can serve to inspire us. There is no such a thing as an overnight success. People who succeed in life have generally been working hard at it for years, before they actually make a success of it. I believe that the secret of success can be summed up in eight words: Hard work, hard work and more hard work.

Task: write down the names of the people who inspire you.

7. Friendship and self-esteem.

A recent radio programme described how the Greek philosopher Aristotle categorised friendship into different types, such as friends who can be helpful to us in practical terms. It seems amazing to me that the different types of friendship that we can have were being talked about and theorised on, that long ago. The fact is we all need friends. No man or woman is an island. The number of friends that we have, is said to peak in our teenage years and early adulthood. How many friends do you need? How many true friends do you actually have?

Paul Grantham in his self-esteem seminar gives a number of reasons why friendship is so important. First, it helps self-acceptance. If someone else really likes us, then we can't be all that bad! Second, it provides us with someone to disclose to. A problem shared is indeed a problem halved. There is no doubt that talking through problems is hugely beneficial. Third, friends can increase our hope and belief in success. They can be good coaches. Fourth, they may encourage us to show the perseverance necessary to tackle certain problems. Fifth, they can reduce our sense of social isolation. Last, they may provide us with extra resources for problem solving, guidance and practical help.

It might be helpful at this point to think about who are the key friends in your own life? Where did you meet them? How long have you known them? Have they helped you out at critical periods in your life? How? Is your relationship with your friends balanced? Are there some friends who take more from you than they give back? Are you happy with your current network of friends? Would you like to make any changes in your friendship network?

Task: Try to draw a map of your friendship and support network. Put yourself in the middle and place around you the key people in your social and personal life.

NURTURING OR ENHANCING YOUR OWN SELF-ESTEEM

To what extent does your ability to make friends rely on your social or communication skills? In the nineteen thirties the American businessman Dale Carnegie wrote the famous book *How to Win Friends and Influence People*. Very few psychologists have ever read this book and even fewer believe that it has much to offer. In a section of the book to do with how we can get people to like us more, Dale Carnegie gives us six tips.

1. Become genuinely interested in other people.
2. Smile.
3. Remember that a person's name is to that person the sweetest and most important sound in any language.
4. Be a good listener. Encourage other people to talk about themselves.
5. Talk in terms of the other person's interests.
6. Make the other person feel important and do it sincerely.

Amazingly some 60 years after this book was written, I attended another self-esteem seminar, this one given by an American psychology professor, Todd Heatherton, he advised us to do five things that research said would help us create a better impression on other people. These were:

1. Smile.
2. Use body language. Try to have open friendly gestures and postures etc.
3. Be a good listener.
4. Take an active interest in the other person.
5. Be positive.

Decades of social psychological research had come up with three of the same five suggestions that Dale Carnegie had, yet Carnegie's suggestions were based solely on his observations of human nature, rather than empirical research. How do you think you add up on these social skills? Either Carnegie's six or Heatherton's five. Is there anything you feel you need to work on in particular?

Task: What social and communication skills do I need to work on?

Of course, one of the things that stops us when we meet new people is that we are often frightened to go up and approach them, without first being introduced. Susan Jeffers addressed this issue in her book, *Dare to Connect*. She complains that each of us has a 'chatterbox' in our heads (called a pathological critic by McKay and Fanning). This stops us approaching other people. Thoughts such as, 'They won't be interested in me,' 'I've got nothing exciting to talk about,' ' I never do well at this sort of thing,' etc. She argues that we need to challenge this negative thinking. Before you approach this person, assure yourself, that no matter what response you get, you are still a worthwhile person. One of her most helpful tips is that you should focus on being *interested* rather than interesting.

Mark Warner talks about the importance of heartprints. This is what you leave when you touch the life of another person. The only way to leave a true heartprint is to be uniquely you and to share with another person the essence of who you are. No masks, no charades, just the real you. Mark argues that the more you can share of yourself, the more unique you become. This can then help you feel more comfortable and personally fulfilled. What sort of impact do you think you have had on other people?

True friends have a very important role in boosting your self-esteem. Conversely some people may have a negative or toxic effect on you. You may need to reconsider how much time you spend with these people if they drag you down. As I suggested earlier with the help of Dale Carnegie, **skills can be important in developing friendship, as are qualities such as trust, authenticity and openness.**

8. Affirmations and self-esteem

Affirmations are positive statements that you can say to yourself on a regular basis. They are especially helpful in counter-acting a lot of the negative messages you may have received earlier in life. They can also be helpful when you have to tackle difficult situations in life. One of the most amazing sets of affirmations that I ever came across was given to me by a woman who attended one of my workshops. She found this set of affirmations written on a postcard in her daughter's handbag, shortly after she died aged 23. These were her affirmations:

> *I'm lovable. I'm worthwhile. I am a courageous black woman and the Mother Spirit shines on me. I am a Black woman of dignity. I am in the present light of the Goddess. She will protect and comfort me.* Cynthia Smith (1971-1994)

Most affirmations are written in the first person and in the present tense eg. 'I take care of myself.' Other affirmations might include the following. 'I am a positive person. I am a good organiser. I am kind to others. I am a good father/mother. I look after my relationships. I can take control of my feelings. I am learning from this experience.' To be maximally effective, affirmations need to become a part of your internal self-talk. It is probably best to have a short list of statements, which you should repeat to yourself many times. Louise Hay gives the affirmation, 'I approve of myself,' to many clients, stating that they need to repeat this three to four hundred times each day. She suggest that this becomes a 'walking mantra.'

There are many ways of drawing up a set of affirmations for each individual. You need to try them all out and see which is the best method for you. Do you need to draw up a short list of brief statements that would provide you with the encouragement you need? A list of affirmations is provided in the appendices. Below, I outline a number of methods for drawing up affirmations.

The first method is by **Jack Canfield,** who pops up throughout this book. His affirmations are quite different from the ones described above. They encourage you to think more about your future goals, and to turn these into your affirmations. He argues that there are eight specific guidelines to follow in drawing up your affirmations.

1. **They must start with the words I am.**
   The words 'I am' are he feels, the most powerful words in any language. He believes that our unconscious takes as a command whatever you say after the words 'I am' to make it come true.

2. **They must be stated positively.**
   Don't say 'I am no longer afraid of snakes.' The unconscious cannot hear a negative, so instead it will hear, 'I am afraid of snakes.' Instead, say 'I am calmly holding a snake.'

3. **State them in the present tense.**
   If you say you are going to lose weight, then you are affirming that you are always on the way to lose weight, not to have actually lost it. Affirm instead that you have already arrived at your weight loss goal.

4. **They need to be brief.**
   If an affirmation is too long, your unconscious cannot remember it.

5. **They must be specific.**
   Don't say 'I am driving my new car,' but 'I am happily driving my new blue Mercedes.'

6. **They should have an –ing word in them.**
   This is so the affirmation is active. The activity will produce the energy that will move the affirmation forward. 'I am proudly cross**ing** the finish line at the London Marathon.'

7. **They should have feeling word in them.**
   Happily, calmly, joyfully etc. The reason you want to achieve a goal is for the feeling it will produce.

8. **They should be about your own life.**
   They should refer to you and not to your partner.

This type of affirmation assumes that we have already reached our goals. In reality, we haven't yet got there. However, each time we state the affirmations our brain becomes aware of this dissonance and tries to take steps to get us there.

Jack suggests that we can have up to 12 affirmations. These should be written onto postcards. He believes that you need to read these three times each day. When you get up in the morning, sometime in the middle of the day and just before bedtime. When you read the affirmations, close your eyes and visualise the results. The purpose of the words is to create a picture. Pictures are more powerful than words. Imagine a picture of you achieving your goal. You may even choose to put some doctored photos of yourself achieving the goal on the other side of the postcard. Two of my own affirmations were, *'I am proudly receiving my PhD at the Barbican,'* and *'I am confidently performing for my black belt grading with Sensei Enoeda.'* The former has now been achieved, but I am still someway short of the second!

Task: Try writing a couple of affirmations for yourself that utilise the above method.

1.

2.

A second type of affirmation strategy that you may wish to consider is that developed by **Nathaniel Branden**. He was the psychologist mentioned in Chapter 1. He uses sentence stems as a way of programming the unconscious to help you move towards healthier self-esteem.

Have a go at some of the following yourself. Take the following sentence stems. Then as rapidly as possible, without pausing for reflection, write as many endings for that sentence as you can in two or three minutes. Never fewer than six, and ten is enough. Do not worry if the endings are literally true or make sense or are profound. Write anything, but write something.

The first stem is:
'If I bring more awareness to my life today....'

1.

2.

3.

4.

5.

6.

Then go onto the next stem:
'If I take more responsibility for my choices and actions today...'

1.

2.

3

4.

5.

6.

NURTURING OR ENHANCING YOUR OWN SELF-ESTEEM

Then:
'If I pay more attention to how I deal with people today...'

1.

2.

3.

4.

5.

6.

Then:
'If I boost my energy level by 5% today ...'

1.

2.

3.

4.

5.

6.

Branden argues that you should do the same exercise every day, Monday to Friday, just before starting work. Once the exercise is finished go about your business as normal. Time spent meditating on these endings helps the creative unconscious to generate connections and insights and to propel growth. Think after the exercise, not during it.

One of my depressed patients was working on the following set of sentence stems:

'If I were to be more positive about the future then...'

'If I could take small steps forward then...'

'If I could congratulate myself on what I achieve today...'

The sort of sentence stems that we might work on, will depend on what our priorities are. Branden has selected stems that fit with his model of self-esteem, which we touched on in Chapter 1, hence he covers issues such as living consciously, self-responsibility etc. For your own purposes, you need to think what you most want to work on. For instance what about the following stems:

'If I listen to my colleagues more today then...'

'If I try and focus on other peoples' good points...'

'If I keep on top of my paperwork...'

'If I treat people the way I want to be treated by them then...'

Task: Have a go at drawing up a couple of sentence stems that might be suitable for some of the goals that you want to work on for yourself.

1.

2.

More details of the sentence completion method can be found in Nathaniel Branden's book *Six Pillars of Self-Esteem*.

NURTURING OR ENHANCING YOUR OWN SELF-ESTEEM

A third method of affirmations is to use the morning and evening power questions of Anthony Robbins. Here, you go over a series of questions before embarking on the day's business and again in the evening. These are taken from his book, *Notes from a Friend*. His **morning power questions** are:

1. What am I happy about in my life right now? What about that makes me happy? How does that make me feel?

2. What am I excited about in my life right now? What about that makes me excited? How does that make me feel?

3. What am I proud of in my life right now? What about that makes me proud? How does that make me feel?

4. What am I grateful for in my life right now? What about that makes me grateful? How does that make me feel?

5. What am I enjoying most in my life right now? What about that makes me enjoy it? How does that make me feel?

6. What am I committed to in my life right now? What about that makes me committed? How does that make me feel?

7. Who do I love? Who loves me? What about that makes me loving? How does that make me feel?

His **evening power questions** are:

1. What have I given today? In what ways have I been a giver today?

2. What did I learn today?

3. How has today added to the quality of my life? How can I use today as an investment in my future?

I have outlined four different methods of affirmations. The first involved selecting or coming up with a brief list of your own positive self-statements that you then repeat to yourself as a 'walking mantra.' The second, was Jack Canfield's goals as affirmations. The third, was Branden's sentence completion method. The last was Anthony

Robbins morning and evening power questions. **Which suits you best? I believe that you have to experiment with all four to see which method suits you best.** Whenever I am facilitating a workshop I have a special affirmation for when the going gets tricky, *'I trust in the workshop process...it will all work out well in the end.'* It hasn't failed yet!

9. Roles and self-esteem

Each of us occupies a variety of social roles in our lives. For instance I occupy the roles of senior lecturer, honorary consultant clinical psychologist, partner, father, grandfather, chairman of a sheltered work charity, brother, nephew, friend etc. That is already 10 different roles. How do your roles contribute to your satisfaction level, and also to your self-esteem? The role mapping exercise, described below, enables us to discover the answers to this question.

Step 1. First put your roles in order of personal priority. These could be as follows:

1. Teacher.
2. Mother.
3. Wife.
4. Grandmother.
5. Sister.
6. and so on until number 10 or however many roles you occupy.

Step 2. Rate each role for satisfaction. A score of 5 shows you are highly satisfied with a particular role. A score of 4 is quite satisfied, 3 is satisfied, 2 is dissatisfied and 1 is very dissatisfied.

Step 3. Rate how much each role contributes to your self-esteem, using the following code.

5 = this role contributes *very considerably* to my self-esteem.
4 = this role contributes *considerably* to my self-esteem.
3 = this role *contributes* to my self-esteem.
2 = this role *does not enhance* my self-esteem.
1 = this role *damages* my self-esteem.

NURTURING OR ENHANCING YOUR OWN SELF-ESTEEM

Task: Complete the role mapping exercise below.

	Role	Satisfaction Level	Contribution to my self-esteem
1.			
2.			
3.			
4.			
5.			
etc.			

This exercise can provide you with a snapshot of all the main roles you occupy in life. It can then highlight where you may need to make changes or where you need to focus your energies. Looking at your own list, how does your work role compare with your role as a parent or partner? Which do you rate as your main priority?

The roles we occupy at present in our lives affect our self-esteem. Having a well paid job, that is also socially valued and personally rewarding, is a great self-esteem booster. Voluntary roles can also bring with them a certain amount of pride. I was previously Chair of Governors at a small infants' school. This role conferred a number of positive advantages on me in terms of status within the school and also the local community. There are undoubtedly many voluntary roles out there for you, which would help boost your self-esteem, if you want to look for them.

10. Stories and self-esteem.

I raised the issue earlier of inspirational figures and role models. Stories can offer insights into many aspects of life. Ruth Stotter comments that

A story may illuminate our relationship to others, encourage compassion, create a sense of wonder or sanction the concept, we are all in this together. A story can make us ponder why we are all here. It may shock us into recognising a new truth, provide a new perspective, a new way to perceive the universe.'

Jack Canfield and his friend Mark Victor Hansen, hit on the idea of the *Chicken Soup for the Soul* series. In this series of books, they edit a collection of stories that help people feel good about themselves and each other. They point out in their introduction to the books that, *'these stories will sustain you in times of challenge, frustration and failure and comfort you in times of confusion, pain and loss.'* They suggest that many of their stories can have some personal meaning for us all. We need to reflect on the stories and see what meaning each may have for us.

Stories as metaphor can also be a powerful learning tool. *Friedman's Fables* is a book that uses the concept of stories as metaphor to teach us important lessons about life. In one of the stories, 'The Bridge', a person is on a journey when they come upon a narrow bridge. They are approached while they are on the bridge by another person, who has a rope around their waist. This person hands one end of the rope to the main protagonist, then proceeds to jump off the bridge! There then ensues a lengthy dialogue between the two characters as to how the person can get back up onto the bridge.

As a professional psychologist, this story is similar to many of the clinical dilemmas that I see in my work. Some patients try and give services the explicit message: 'if you don't help me, then I'm going to let go of the rope and kill myself.' The person with an addiction may ask for help with their problems, but is unwilling to take responsibility for their own actions. They are unwilling to climb up the rope themselves. Friedman states that **the moral of this story, is that as soon as you think you have life worked out, it has a habit of throwing some obstacle in your path!**

How might stories relate to your sense of self-esteem? Well, we can learn from factual accounts how other people may have coped with similar adversity to that which you are perhaps experiencing. Stories as metaphor can provide a different insight into an issue. In

NURTURING OR ENHANCING YOUR OWN SELF-ESTEEM

the story of 'The Apple, Pear and Plum,' an old man tries to get a young child to say which of the three trees produces the best fruit and is therefore the best tree. After resisting much cajoling from the old man, the child says that each tree has its own merits and that none is better than the other. The message is, so are you. Sometimes society values one attribute higher than another, yet it doesn't mean that we are not all equally talented, just in different ways.

Barry Lopez, amongst others, suggests that stories have a very powerful function for humankind. He states:

The stories people tell have a way of taking care of them. If stories come to you, care for them, and learn to give them away when needed. Sometimes a person needs a story more than food to stay alive. That is why we put stories into each other's memories. That is how people care for themselves.

In their book, *The Path of the Everyday Hero* Lorna Catford and Michael Ray, compare each of our life's journeys to a hero's journey. They suggest that each of us is confronted by five major challenges in life. These are:

1. Discovering and pursuing your true purpose.

2. Bringing love into your life.

3. Living stress free in the here and now.

4. Achieving personal and professional balance.

5. Finding your way to prosperity.

Their book provides an experiential guide on how to progress through each of these dimensions.

> *A disciple once complained, 'You tell us stories, but you never reveal their meaning to us.' The master replied, 'How would you like it if someone offered you fruit and chewed it up for you before giving it to you.* (Anon)

11. Feedback and self-esteem.

In developing any skill, feedback is a critical element. It lets you know how you are doing. It lets you know what is working and what isn't. In personal matters, giving feedback to a colleague or friend can be difficult. Any hint of criticism often makes people defensive and may even provoke an angry response back. I was once asked by my line manager to tell a student about their strong body odour. How do you think I gave that feedback? Easy. I didn't! However, there are times when you have no alternative but to give feedback. So how can you best do this, while at the same time being careful not to upset someone's sense of self-esteem?

Years ago, I worked with a number of American psychiatric rehabilitation experts. The main aim of their work was to try and improve the social skills of people with long term mental health problems. To do this, they used a variety of techniques, which can be loosely described as social skills training. Conversation skills were broken down into five core component skills:

1. verbal and nonverbal behaviour,
2. starting a conversation,
3. maintaining conversations,
4. ending conversations, and then
5. putting it all together.

Each of these five core skills was taught in the same systematic way, starting with a video demonstration, followed by actual practice of the skill with role play and coaching. Having watched the patient perform the skill, the coach then had to give feedback. The way you do this, is by commenting on four or five good points that you liked about the performance. Having done this, you would then select one area where you felt the patient needed to work on. The conversation would go something like this, *'I wonder if I could now show you one area where I feel you could improve on.'* You would then specify what they needed to do and what that behaviour was. When you express behaviours that the person needs to change in terms of something that they can improve on, it avoids the in-built defensiveness that negative feedback can provoke. At the end of the day, how would you rather be told about some skill of yours that needed working on? **What approach do you think would be better for your own self-esteem?** This issue of how we give feedback to others also touches on the metaphor of the dipper and the bucket, which I will return to in the last chapter.

12. Happiness and self-esteem.

I spend my entire professional life listening to many people who have long term depressive illnesses. They are not happy people. In recent years, there has been an attempt to try and promote happiness as an antidote to much of the depression that seems to pervade modern life. The BBC even sponsored a series to try and make the people of Slough happier. Dr Tim Sharp is one of many writers that has written on this subject. He has provided a very helpful e-booklet with a number of tips on how you can become a happier person (see: http://www.thehappinessinstitute.com). These are his tips:

1. make happiness a priority,
2. make plans for it,
3. set happy goals,
4. do things that make you happy,
5. set tasks that will give you satisfaction,
6. play and have fun,
7. identify your strengths,
8. utilise your strengths,
9. be curious,
10. be grateful and appreciate what you have,
11. learn to like and ideally love yourself,
12. invest time and energy in your key relationships,
13. live a healthy life,
14. ensure you get adequate sleep and rest,
15. manage your time and priorities,
16. control what you can control,

17. socialise and interact with others as much as possible,

18. weed out unhelpful thoughts,

19. plant happier thoughts,

20. live in the present moment,

21. make happiness an integral part of your life.

(See also *The Happiness Handbook*, by Dr Tim Sharp).

Most of these suggestions have been covered in other sections of this chapter. It seems obvious to state that when you are happy, the chances are that your levels of self-esteem will be higher. Conversely, when you are depressed, then the likelihood is that your levels of self-esteem will plummet. This focus on happiness coincides with a new movement in psychology called Positive Psychology. My only caveat, is that life is full of both ups and downs and as I mentioned earlier in Kahlil Gibran's words, 'Joy and Sorrow.' Some people are dealt a much worse deck of cards to play the game of life with and naturally this colours their perceptions. For them happiness may seem like an illusion or a delusion. **There is no doubt that being happy helps our self-esteem,** but you need to accept that at certain times, such as following the death of someone close to you, that this may not always be possible and that it really is alright for you to be sad. Indeed sadness is a normal part of the grieving process.

13. Building on your strengths.

Along with the move towards a more positive approach to psychology, there has been increasing emphasis on helping build up people's strengths. Ironically, when we see people in clinical settings, we always start our sessions by having them tell us all about their problems. There is no explicit section in my initial interview format that asks people about their strengths. Yet it is their strengths that are going to help them get back onto the road of mental well-being.

In *Now Discover Your Strengths* Marcus Buckingham and Donald Clifford describe a systematic approach to focussing on each of our strengths. They challenge the fact that a lot of organisations focus their training efforts on two flawed assumptions. First, that individuals are capable of being competent in most areas of work. Second, that their room for most growth is in their areas of weakness. Instead, they argue that we need to be focussing on concentrating and developing individual talents and strengths to maximise their contribution to the organisation. Through years of research on behalf of the Gallup organisation, they have identified 34 different human talents that we all vary on. To discover your own unique list of talents, you will however need to purchase a copy of their book, which contains a code to enable you to take their Internet *StrengthsFinder Profile Test.* This will help you discover your own five dominant or signature themes. For what it's worth my five are:

1. Maximiser (strengths, whether yours or someone else's fascinate you).

2. Achiever (a constant need for achievement).

3. Learner (you love the process of learning).

4. Context (you look back to understand the present).

5. Empathy (you can sense the emotions of those around you).

The key to their approach is to identify your dominant themes and then develop these.

Certainly, I have been intrigued how some people have been able to make a huge success out of their talents (I would do being a Maximiser myself!). Witness the success of the celebrity chefs Jamie Oliver and Gordon Ramsey. Look at football pundits like Alan Hansen or rugby commentators such as Jonathan Davies. Wedded to an undoubted talent in their own specific sport, they are also natural and skilled communicators. Yet each of us has our own talents.

Task: What do you think are your main talents? Does your job offer you an opportunity to use these talents to their full? What is it that you enjoy doing most in life, that when you are doing it, you can't wait to get back and do it again?

Each of us needs to find those unique areas that we are most gifted in. If you can find the right outlet for your own talents, who knows what you can achieve? **Building on our strengths helps build up our self-esteem.**

Summary

A **good self-esteem programme needs to nurture or enhance the self-esteem of participants**, the third of Mruk's objectives. In this chapter I have outlined 13 different areas that connect to enhancing our self-esteem. You need to improve your sense of self-worth and develop your level of personal competence. Some of my suggestions are geared more towards your sense of self-worth eg. cognitive behaviour therapy, others are more directly linked to personal competence such as finding your strengths. Hopefully, if you are now working on some of these areas we can now move onto our next chapter which considers how to maintain the gains in self-esteem.

> *The good man does not grieve that other people do not recognise his merits. His only anxiety is lest he should fail to recognise theirs.* Confucius.

FOUR

MAINTAINING YOUR LEVEL OF SELF-ESTEEM

Concerning all acts of initiative and creation, there is one elemental truth - the ignorance of which kills countless ideas and splendid plans: that the moment one definitely commits oneself, the Providence moves too. All sorts of things occur to help one that would never otherwise have occurred. Goethe.

In this penultimate chapter, I consider ways of ensuring that your level of self-esteem can be maintained.

1. The importance of goals

In his classic text, *Man's Search for Meaning,* the psychiatrist Viktor Frankl talked about his life in a concentration camp during World War 2. Frankl noticed that the people who survived were not the fittest, healthiest or most intelligent individuals. The survivors were those individuals who had goals. Goals are what keep you going. In his book, *Follow Your Heart: Finding Purpose in Your Life and Work,* Andrew Matthews states that none of us can manage without goals. What is important is not so much the nature of the goal you have, just as long as you have a goal. Matthews cites Buckminster Fuller and his Law of Precession. This is the principle that you will gain many things in addition to the goal itself. The most important thing is not the actual goal, but what you learn and how much you grow and develop along the way. Your goal in going to college may be to get an academic qualification. However, you will also gain a lot socially from meeting lots of new people and having many enriching experiences along the way.

Having goals is essential if you are to improve and maintain your self-esteem. There are many ways of choosing goals and one way is to use the **SMART** principle. That is, a goal needs to be:

Specific

Measurable

Achievable

Realistic

Timed

Saying that 'you want to get fitter' is not a SMART goal. On the other hand, if I stated that 'I am going to get fitter by attending twice weekly karate classes over the next six months,' this is specific, measurable, achievable, realistic and has a time frame.

Task: Draw up two goals that will enhance your self-esteem:

I am going to……

I am going to…..

2. Obstacles that get in the way of change

If it were easy to change your attitudes and behaviour, you would have done so by now! In considering the two or three goals you are going to be working on to enhance your self-esteem, you need to be aware of the potential obstacles that could possibly derail you. Let's say that I have decided to lose weight from my current weight of 16 stone, down to a target weight of 12½ stone. This will not only enhance my self-esteem as I will look much better, but it clearly has a lot of health benefits. I only need to really do two things. One is to reduce my calorific intake and to eat healthier less fattening foods. The second is to increase my level of exercise so I am using up more calories that I am now. What could possibly go wrong?

Choosing weight is a good behaviour change target, as there is a clear behavioural product to measure, weight! You could say 'your waistline' as well! Most weight loss classes start with all the class being weighed. I need therefore to start monitoring my weight on a least a weekly basis, so I can see how I'm progressing, and if all the hard work I am putting in is paying off. Here I hit my first obstacle, as we don't have a decent set of scales at home! The first step needs to be investing in a set of scales! Luckily, there is a group of staff at work, all on diets, and I am being monitored along with them.

Food is of course a great comforter. Without even realising it, you may reach out for a snack when rushed or stressed. When we need a drink, what do we choose? Often after training hard, I would drink a couple of 'high energy' drinks, having been taken in by the advertising that these replenish your energy supplies. I would have been much better off drinking water! The obvious solution to our stressed busy lifestyles might seem to be fast food, for people who don't have much time to stop and eat. Yet as many of you will know, fast food can in itself be quite unhealthy.

There are a number of strategies that you can utilise to help you deal with obstacles to change. Some of them are illustrated in the tasks overleaf:

Tasks

- **Work on your goal with someone else**, who is also keen to tackle that problem eg. join a weight loss class with a friend. You can then encourage each other.

- **Put a list of your goals** on your fridge, by your computer, on your desk at work, in your diary etc. Try using the method of goals as affirmations described by Jack Canfield in the last chapter.

- **Share your goals** with other people in your life. Encourage them to ask you how you are progressing.

- **Reward yourself for progress** made towards achieving your goals.

The more progress you make to achieving your goals, the stronger your sense of personal agency and control will become. This will enhance your self-esteem at the same time.

MAINTAINING YOUR LEVEL OF SELF-ESTEEM

3. Enhancing your sense of wellness

Paul Wilson, author of *Calm for Life,* advises that you can do six things to enhance your sense of personal wellness. The better we feel in ourselves, the more likely we are to have high self-esteem. These are his tips:

1. **Look after your diet.**
   We've been here before! Paul stresses the importance of maintaining an alkaline-acid balance in the foods you eat in the ratio of 80:20. He also recommends that we eat foods as close to the way nature intended ie. unprocessed foods as much as possible.

2. **Enjoy exercise.**
   Personally, I rarely found going to the gym to be very enjoyable, granted it was quite a run down gym! Looking around, few others seemed to be having much fun either. Paul states that we all need to exercise for a minimum of 30 to 45 minutes, five times a week. That's the bad news. The good news is that walking is the most relaxing exercise programme available and we can all do more walking without making dramatic changes to our lifestyles.

3. **Develop a positive attitude.**
   Paul states that most optimists succeed, most pessimists fail. He may be slightly exaggerating the point here, but there is no doubt as we saw in the last chapter that optimists are healthier, wealthier and happier than pessimists. He also emphasises the importance of humour. *Reader's Digest* has run a column for decades called, 'Laughter the best medicine,' which was also epitomised in the film *Patch Adams,* by a doctor who used humour as a large part of his practice of medicine.

4. **Love what you do.**
   Putting more effort and focus into our everyday life, means we will get more out of what we do. Paul argues that we should strive to make even everyday tasks, like cleaning, a meditation, so we get more out of them.

5. **Help others.**
   Paul stresses the need to find the good in others. Great people help other people to become great. Small people try to hold

other people back. Engaging in voluntary work, where we give something back for no monetary gain, can give us all pleasure.

6. **Learn to become calm.**
   You wouldn't expect the guru of calm to advocate anything else. Paul stresses the long term health benefits of regular meditation practice.

Task: Commit to doing at least two of the six things listed above to improve your sense of wellness.

I am going to work on_____

I am going to work on_____

4. Resources to help boost your self-esteem

I mentioned earlier that there were almost 3,000 *books* on the topic of self-esteem, not to mention the thousands more general titles in the self-help genre. Big bookshops are awash with these titles, though there is an even wider selection via on-line bookshops such as Amazon.com on the Internet.

Audio cassettes now already being replaced by CDs, can also be very helpful in assisting with the coaching process. I have listened to several of these, but if I had to pick out one, it would be Jack Canfield's *Self-Esteem and Peak Performance*. I have mentioned his work several times in this book.

All of these resources are available via the *Internet*. The Net is becoming an increasingly important resource and for me is often the first port of call when I want to find the latest information on any topic.

Librarians are another resource available to you in your quest for information. If I ever need a literature review to be conducted, I always ask a librarian. They know how to access all the relevant databases that may be relevant to your topic. Your local library will have information sources that you won't realise unless you are already a regular visitor.

Friends are of course another resource. You may want to ask them if they have come across any inspiring information on the topic. It is amazing how when someone asks you about a topic, suddenly you start looking out for information on that topic and begin to notice additional material. Just yesterday I was listening to a Radio 4 presentation on their book of the week. This was a serialisation of the biography of the playwright John Osborne. I recalled that I had also read excerpts from this in the Guardian Review section. It reminded me of the relationship he had with his daughter. He had actually written to her detailing his innermost feelings about her, and how awful he felt towards her. I found myself wondering what effect this must have had on his daughter's self-esteem. The daughter was rescued by a kindly vicar and his family, who became her surrogate father.

The point I would make, is that there are lots of resources out there which will help maintain you in your quest for a healthier self-esteem.

Task: I am going to seek out the following information to do with my self-esteem.

5. Stigma and self-esteem.

I mentioned the case earlier of the young man with dyslexia. I remember when I did workshops in the Midlands for a social services department, that a number of staff raised the issue of racism and how it affected their collective sense of self-esteem. Events such as Black History Month are designed to inform the wider debate on the positive contribution that many black people have made to society. Many of us will have been taught at school about the heroic work of Florence Nightingale in the Crimea in the nineteenth century. Yet how many of you will have read about Mary Seacole, a black nurse who was equally important. Fortunately, more and more educational materials in schools are culturally sensitive and hopefully in years to come, future generations will be much more culturally tolerant. Again being gay, mentally ill or having a physical disability can also affect individual's self-esteem, though this is often more due to people's reactions towards diversity. One gay man in one of my workshops played a scene from an American film where a gay man told his mother about his sexuality. Her reaction was telling and very damaging to his sense of identity. The man went onto say how his own parents had reacted when he 'came out' about his own sexuality.

Many of the people that I work with have been given a diagnosis of schizophrenia. One young man I know often tells people this shortly after he meets them. In the majority of cases the word 'schizophrenia' conjures up notions of split personality and images of 'mad axemen.' Indeed some of our patients feel moved to reassure members of the public after they have learned of their mental illness, 'Don't worry, I'm not violent!.' While a lot of TV soap programmes have tried to present mental illness in a more positive and normal light, most people still have a negative image of severe mental illness. Films like *A Beautiful Mind* with Russell Crowe can play a major part in helping educate the public about such conditions. Again, stories of recovery from major mental disorder can give hope to sufferers. There are also a number of individuals in this country such as Ron Coleman, Peter Chadwick and Rufus May, who have all had psychosis and have made full recoveries. These people bear powerful witness to what can be achieved, despite the individuals having suffered with serious mental disorder. Membership of any minority or disadvantaged group can have an adverse effect on members' self-esteem.

Task: I am going to read or watch something about how an individual has coped with disadvantage or disability.

6. Still the body, calm the mind

Paul Wilson stresses the benefit of meditation. The American psychologist John Kabat-Zinn has introduced meditation practice into the American healthcare system. Patients with a variety of physical conditions ranging from coronary problems to cancer are offered group meditation practice alongside conventional medical treatments. In Britain, Professor Mark Williams and Professor John Teasdale are using mindfulness based cognitive therapy to treat individuals with long term recurrent depressive illnesses. Mindfulness meditation is a key element of this approach and individuals are required to practice meditation for at least 45 minutes every day. These approaches are essentially trying to still the body and through this to calm the mind. Yoga practice can have an equal benefit for health. There is no doubt that the National Health Service is underutilising the potential of approaches such as yoga and meditation, and over-emphasizing physical treatments such as drugs. Patients seeking such treatments are often advised to find them outside the NHS and have to pay for them privately. There is no doubt of the benefits of both yoga and meditation. Daily practice will help you feel better in yourself and is more likely to lead you to have better self-esteem.

Task: I am going to spend 30 minutes each day relaxing or meditating.

7. Having a 'feel good' or 'warm and fuzzy file'

One of the techniques that Jack Canfield recommends for maintaining your self-esteem is having a warm and fuzzy file. (If the phrase grates on you, then choose another name for it, such as a 'feel good' folder). I have a large box file. In this, I put all the cards, letters, testimonials etc that I have received which say nice things about me. Whenever each of us feels low or depressed, this is the time to get out the file and read the positive things that other people have said about us. It is amazing how you can forget about some of the contents of the file, until you go over the items again. It can also contain photos, postcards, essentially anything that will help remind you of happier times and that has a positive personal message for you. You may think that you have little in the way of positive feedback from other people. At Christmas, or on your birthday, amongst the cards you receive, one or two people may have said a little more in their cards. They may have thanked you for some favour you did for them, or for being there for them when they had a personal crisis. These are the sorts of things that you need to save for your 'warm and fuzzy' file. Over time these will build up and you will probably need a second box file! Don't throw these things away, but rather use them as a tool to help maintain your self-esteem! A common exercise I use at the end of my self-esteem workshops, is that I get participants, who have generally spent three days together working in the same small groups, to write short positive messages in cards for each member of their small group. When the task is completed, I have them read all their cards to themselves. Individuals are often surprised at the positive things that others have said about them. One young occupational therapist who attended my first ever self-esteem workshop, said that no one had ever written such nice things about him before! If you are working with a group who know each other very well, then they can be asked to write something about the whole group! It is critical that everyone writes something positive.

Task: Make up your own 'feel good' or 'warm and fuzzy' file, or call it by any other name you prefer.

To my mind, this is one of the most helpful practical things you can do which will help maintain your sense of self-esteem in the future. Don't worry if you don't have much to put in it at first. Trust me, it will build up over time!

8. Filling buckets.

I introduced the filling buckets metaphor earlier in this book. I was amazed to discover that the metaphor had been expanded into a book, *How Full is your Bucket?* by Tom Rath and Donald Clifton. To reiterate the concept, this is how they describe the metaphor:

> *Everyone has an invisible bucket. We are at our best when our buckets are overflowing- and at our worst when they are empty. Everyone also has an invisible dipper (ladle). In each interaction we can use our dipper either to fill or to dip from others' buckets. Whenever we choose to fill other's buckets, we in turn fill our own.*

Regular bucket filling can increase positive emotions. Dr Barbara Fredrickson of the University of Michigan, argues that positive emotions are important because:

- They protect from, and can reverse the effects of, negative emotions.

- They build resilience and can change people.

- They expand thinking and can encourage problem solving.

- They can break down cultural barriers.

- They build durable personal resources that can act as 'reserves' in difficult times.

- They produce optimal functioning in organisations and individuals.

- They improve the overall performance of a group when its leaders express more positive emotions.

Rath and Clifton argue that it would not harm us to go on a diet consisting of more positive emotions and fewer negative emotions. They suggest there are five ways to increase positive emotions:

1. Prevent bucket dipping, both your own and others.

2. Shine a light on what is right. Start praising your colleagues and friends.

3. Make best friends with people you come into contact with.

4. Give unexpectedly. Look for opportunities to give small gifts to others out of the blue.

5. Reverse the golden rule. 'Do unto others as they would have you do unto them.' Individualise your recognition. That is, different individuals like to be praised in unique ways. For instance some prefer a quiet word of thanks, others would rather a more public announcement etc.

This is part of a new movement in psychology, that is called Positive Psychology, the study of what is right with people. Self-esteem is consistent with this positive approach.

Task: Make a conscious attempt to fill at least two peoples' buckets each day over the next week.

9. The attitude of gratitude.

You have just been for a wonderful dinner party at a friend's house. Do you ever drop them a short note to thank them? One of your colleagues makes a special effort to help you out at work. Do you drop them a thank you note? As a nation, it is said that the British send more cards per head than any other nation. E-mail is changing this of course. We may often e-mail our thanks, rather than going out to buy a special card.

Showing appreciation for the things that other people do for us, takes comparatively little physical effort, yet it is almost always deeply appreciated. I was once at a function at Dulwich Picture Gallery. It was an event to celebrate 50 years of the Institute of Psychiatry's clinical psychology training course. It brought together people who had trained on the course over that entire period. I noticed that a senior manager from the Trust was on his own and that very few people seemed to be talking to him. Clearly people were renewing acquaintances with friends they hadn't seen for years, and not being a psychologist he was being left out. I made a deliberate effort to introduce this senior manager to several people and thought nothing much of it at the time. I felt this was merely a polite thing to do. The next week I was amazed to receive a hand-written letter from him, thanking me for my consideration. He clearly knew all about cultivating the attitude of gratitude, to borrow another of Jack Canfield's phrases.

How often do *you* thank people for things they have done for you?

Task: Write and thank someone for something that they did for you recently. Make a conscious effort to thank people more for what they have done for you.

10. Poetry, music and stories to inspire

I have never met Daisy Goodwin before. However I have seen her present the series *Essential Poems* on BBC2. I have also bought several of her books on poetry including, *101 Poems that Could Save Your Life,'* and *'101 Poems to Keep You Sane*. In one of her most recent books, *Poems to Last a Lifetime*, she states

> use this book as a recipe for life: turn to it when you need some advice on everything from growing up to getting old; look to it for consolation when the phone doesn't ring or for inspiration when you are trying to do the right thing ...

Poetry has a way of connecting to something deep within us, that moves us in a way that prose can sometimes fail to do. When combined with film it can be incredibly powerful. Many of you may remember the funeral scene from the film *Four Weddings and a Funeral*. The bereaved partner stands up and says the following lines,

> He was my North, my South, my East and West,
> My working week and my Sunday rest.

Yet not many people will have realised that these are lines from W.H. Auden's poem, 'Funeral Blues.' One of the participants in a workshop introduced me to the poet Kahlil Gibran, and his book *The Prophet*. This has several poems which touch on a lot of the key issues in life, such as love, work, family, friendship, beauty etc. They speak to the mystery of life. There are no doubt many poems which will have a resonance and meaning for you. A poem like 'Joy and Sorrow' reminds us all that life is full of ups and downs and that we should expect no less.

Music is another medium that can inspire us all. In my three day self-esteem workshops I ask participants to give a brief presentation on the final day, related to the topic of self-esteem. I hand them emergency guidelines on Day 1 to help get them over the panic that knowing you have to give a presentation can elicit. The default option that I give them, is that they can simply choose a piece of music or poetry that has helped them feel better about themselves. Over the years I have heard lots of different music played in these slots, which has the capacity to lift and inspire, ranging from Buena Vista Social Club to Tasmin Archer and many more musicians in-between. So many lyrics seem to capture the same experiences and emotions that we all feel and at times it can seem as if a particular song has a special resonance for us. I used to play the REM song, 'Everybody Hurts' after completing the Graph of Life Satisfaction, again as a way of saying, we all have downs in life and it can be very painful.

Task: Write down the poetry and music that inspire you. Make an effort to reconnect with these media and to remind yourself of the messages they contained.

How often do we read stories in the newspapers or magazines that inspire us? I remember a very inspirational piece by the journalist Decca Aitkenhead, which appeared in the *Guardian* Saturday Supplement. This described how her father, brother and sisters coped with the death of her mother from cancer, when she was a child. She related how her family were told every single detail of their mother's condition and what would happen to her, as she lay dying at home, except one thing. That it would hurt! We need to hold onto narratives like this, as they have important lessons about life, that can help us or those close to us when we face similar troubles in life.

I once attended a one day workshop on Inspirational Leadership, which used Shakespeare's Henry V as an example of how to inspire people. The facilitators used two specific passages to great effect, especially since the lecturer was able to say the passages from heart and proclaimed them in the manner of a professional actor on stage. One was during the siege of Harfleur and is from Act Three Scene 1. I quote some lines below,

> *Stiffen the sinews, summon up the blood,*
> *Disguise fair nature with hard-favoured rage,*
>
> *Follow your spirit, and upon this charge,*
> *Cry, 'God, for Harry, England and Saint George*

Again just before the battle of Agincourt, when the English troops were massively outnumbered by the French forces, Shakespeare has

BE YOUR OWN SELF-ESTEEM COACH

Henry saying some of the following words,

> *The fewer men, the greater the share of honour....*
> *From this day to the ending of the world*
> *But we in it shall be remembered,*
> *We few, we happy few, we band of brothers;...*
> *And gentlemen in England now abed*
> *Shall thinks themselves accursed they were not here,*
> *And hold their manhoods cheap whiles any speaks*
> *That fought with us on St.Crispin's day.*

MAINTAINING YOUR LEVEL OF SELF-ESTEEM

Task: Start making an effort to collect inspiring stories that you come across in the papers or magazines.

11. Tips from experts

Titus Alexander in *The Self-Esteem Directory* provides a list of tips for self-esteem enhancement. These are his tips:

1. You are a wonderful, worthwhile, capable, lovable person. Your job is to get in touch with this reality about yourself.

2. Get in touch with positive feelings. Remember things you have achieved and times that you felt valued in life. Imagine, remember and savour those moments.

3. Cancel negative self-talk. Link negative thoughts with a positive eg. 'I may feel insecure, but I am still a worthwhile person.'

4. Celebrate the fact you are you!

5. List things you can do and positive qualities about yourself.

6. Complete the past. List every unfinished task and either finish it now, set a date when you will finish it, or give it up.

7. Learn from negative experiences.

8. Join an affirming process or activity. Find an activity to do with people who value you, find positive people who give you encouraging feedback.

9. Look out some self-help books and tapes.

10. Give thanks to people who have done things for you in the past or recently.

I obtained a second set of tips from a website on the Internet. This listed 13 ways to increase your self-esteem. These are:

1. Build your confidence. Visualise yourself succeeding at tasks.

2. Reach out to others. Help others more.
3. Avoid perfectionism.
4. Take care of your physical appearance.
5. Get in touch with your own creative energy.
6. Respect your self. What would friends who admire you say about you?
7. Look for a silver lining.
8. Act in accordance with your own values.
9. Be good to yourself on a daily basis.
10. Challenge yourself.
11. Practice optimism.
12. Don't take things so personally.
13. Don't take things so seriously.

Summary

In this chapter we have looked at ways of **maintaining your level of self-esteem,** ranging from making up your own warm and fuzzy file, to practicing meditation. You need to find the methods that appeal most to you. Attending workshops can provide you with a great lift and a real desire to get started. However it is important that the momentum for change is kept up. Goethe's words at the start of this chapter are true. Once you definitely commit yourself to a course of action, all sorts of things occur to help you, that otherwise would never have occurred.

> *The tragedy is that so many people look for self-confidence and self-respect everywhere except within themselves, and so they fail in their search.* Nathaniel Branden

FIVE

CONCLUDING COMMENTS

It is not the critic who counts ; not the man who points out how the strong man stumbled, or where the doer of deeds could have done them better. The credit belongs to the man who is actually in the arena. Theodore Roosevelt

While this chapter signals the end of the book, it is really only the start of the process. We all read books, then place them back on the shelf, seldom to be reopened again. You cannot afford to do this with your self-esteem. The business of enhancing and maintaining our self-esteem is an on-going process. It does not have an end. Just as our self-esteem will rise, so will it fall. However, if you have followed the tips in this book, this will help even out the fluctuations. You might reasonably ask, of all the techniques and methods mentioned in this book, which is the most effective or important one. The answer, is the one that works best for you. No one technique will work on its own. It will require a combination of techniques. Sometimes just having a heightened awareness of the issue of self-esteem, is sufficient to start the process of change. Let me recap the main points for you that I have attempted to cover in the book.

First, why you need to *Be Your Own Self-Esteem Coach*. In the Introduction I mentioned that at certain stages in life we may only have ourselves. You may be the only person you can rely on. It is critical therefore that you become your own best friend and have a positive view of yourself.

Second, I have shown in Chapter 1 that self-esteem comprises two main elements- self-worth and personal competence. To tackle the issue of self-esteem you need to work on both elements. Individuals with high self-esteem are more likely to take more risks in life and are therefore more likely to get more out of what life has to offer.

This has hopefully helped you **to better understand the concept of self-esteem.**

Third, in Chapter 2, I helped develop your understanding of what developmental factors influenced your own self-esteem. Drawing a graph of your life satisfaction highlights the effects of major life events on your own life. Completing the Rosenberg Self-Esteem Scale showed your current level of self-esteem. This Chapter **has enabled you to get a better understanding of your own self-esteem.**

Fourth, in Chapter 3, I outlined 13 different ways of nurturing or enhancing your own self-esteem. These were by:

- valuing your own personal achievements.
- appreciating and developing your personal resilience.
- understanding the link between self-image and self-esteem.
- testing your level of optimism and by realising the benefits of having an optimistic approach.
- seeing the links between negative thinking and low self-esteem.
- being able to derive inspiration from role models.
- appreciating the value of friends for your self-esteem.
- developing affirmations that will enhance your self-esteem and lead to behaviour change.
- considering how the social roles you occupy affect your self-esteem.
- learning how true stories and stories as metaphor can provide helpful lessons in your self-esteem journey.
- learning how to give feedback to others that nurtures their self-esteem.
- seeing how being happier can help.
- focussing on your unique talents.

These are all ways **to nurture and enhance your own self-esteem.**

Finally, in Chapter 4, I presented eleven **ways to maintain your level of self-esteem**. These were by:

- drawing up goals to work on.
- being aware of obstacles to change.
- enhancing your sense of wellness.
- using resources to assist you.
- learning how stigma can affect your self-esteem.

CONCLUDING COMMENTS

- relaxation and meditation.
- starting up your own warm and fuzzy file.
- filling other people's buckets.
- cultivating the attitude of gratitude.
- using poetry, music and stories to inspire you.
- learning tips from experts in the field.

Finally, there are many good books out there that can help you on your journey through life. The writer Paulo Coelho author of *The Alchemist,* is one of many authors who uses metaphor to teach important lessons. You will have your own idea of books that have inspired and continue to inspire you. My final set of tips for you is from Hal Urban. After his wife left him, Hal wanted to write a book about the important issues in life for his sons. The book, *Life's Greatest Lessons: 20 Things that Matter,* became a best seller in the States. These are his 20 lessons:

1. Life is hard…and not always fair.
2. Life is also fun … and incredibly funny.
3. Success is more than making money.
4. We live by choice, not by chance.
5. Attitude is a choice-the most important one you'll ever make.
6. Habits are the key to all success.
7. Being thankful is a habit- the best one you'll ever have.
8. Good people live their lives on a foundation of respect.
9 Honesty is still the best policy.
10. Kind words cost little but accomplish much.
11. Real motivation comes from within.
12. Goals are dreams with deadlines.
13. There's no substitute for hard work.
14. You have to give up something to get something.
15. Successful people don't find time, they make time.
16. No one else can raise your self-esteem.
17. The body need nutrition and exercise, so do the mind and spirit.
18. It's okay to fail. Everyone else has.
19. Life is simpler when we know what is essential.
20. Essential number one is being a good person.

There is a clear overlap with many of the suggestions from this book. Though if there were one tip that summed up this book, it would be number 16, **no one else can raise your self-esteem**, apart from YOU!

BE YOUR OWN SELF-ESTEEM COACH

Our deepest fear is not that we are inadequate.
Our deepest fear is that we are powerful beyond measure.
It is our light not our darkness that frightens us.
We ask ourselves. Who am I to be brilliant, gorgeous, talented and fabulous?
Actually, who are we not to be?
Your playing small doesn't serve the world.
There is nothing enlightened about shrinking so that other people won't feel insecure around you.
As we let our own light shine,
We unconsciously give other people permission to do the same.
As we are liberated from our fear, our presence automatically liberates others. Nelson Mandela.

REFERENCES

BRANDEN, Nathaniel (1994) *The Six Pillars of Self-Esteem*. Bantam, New York

FENNELL, Melanie (1999) *Overcoming Low Self-Esteem*. Robinson, London

FIELD, Lynda (1995) *The Self-Esteem Workbook*. Element, Shaftesbury, Dorset

MRUK, Christopher (1999) *Self-Esteem: Research, Theory and Practice*. Springer, New York

URBAN, Hal (2003) *Life's Greatest Lessons: Twenty Things That Matter*. Fireside, Simon and Schuster, New York

WARNER, Mark (1999) *The Complete Idiot's Guide to Self-Esteem*. Alpha Books, New York

APPENDIX ONE

SELF-ESTEEM QUOTATIONS

A person's worth in this world, is estimated according to the value they put on themselves.
Jean de la Bruyère

Aerodynamically the bumblebee shouldn't be able to fly, but the bumblebee doesn't know that so it keeps on flying anyway.
Mary Kay Ash

Trust yourself, then you will know how to live.
Goethe

Let the world know you as you are, not as you think you should be, because sooner or later, if you are posing, you will forget the pose, and then where are you.
Fanny Brice

We visit others as a matter of social obligation. How long has it been since we have visited with ourselves?
Morris Adler

Nurses might recognise that there lies within the practice of nursing a deceptively subtle phenomenon- called care- that is still waiting to be developed. Few other disciplines have much time for care- indeed many believe foolishly, that it is lowly unskilled practice- indeed that it might even be just women's work.
Phil Barker

The tragedy of life does not lie in not reaching your goals, the tragedy lies in not having any goals to reach.
Benjamin Mays

BE YOUR OWN SELF-ESTEEM COACH

First thing every morning before you arise say out loud, 'I believe' three times.
Norman Vincent Peale

We wait all these years to find someone who understands us, I thought, someone who accepts us as we are, someone with a wizard's power to melt stone to sunlight, who can bring us happiness in spite of trials, who can face our dragons in the night, who can transform us into the soul we choose to be. Just yesterday I found that magical Someone is the face we see in the mirror; It's us and our homemade masks.
Richard Bach

Outstanding leaders go out of their way to boost the self-esteem of their personnel. If people believe in themselves, it's amazing what they can accomplish.
Sam Walton

Nothing builds self-esteem and self-confidence like accomplishment.
Thomas Carlyle

Know yourself. Trust yourself, be yourself.
Greg Dyke

Seek out that particular mental attribute which makes you feel most deeply and vitally alive, along with which comes the inner voice which says, 'This is the real me,' and when you have found that attitude, follow it.
James Adams

I am sure it is one's duty as a teacher to try to show boys that no opinions, no tastes, no emotions are worth much unless they are one's own. I suffered acutely as a boy from the lack of being shown this.
AC Benson

If you put a small value on yourself, rest assured that the world will not raise your price.
Anon

Argue for your limitations and sure enough they're yours.
Richard Bach

APPENDIX ONE: SELF-ESTEEM QUOTATIONS

You cannot be lonely if you like the person you're alone with.
Wayne Dyer

The will to do springs from the knowledge that we can do.
James Allen

You have to leave the city of your comfort and go into the wilderness of your intuition. What you'll discover will be wonderful. What you'll discover will be yourself.
Alan Alda

When an archer misses the mark, he turns and looks for the fault within himself. Failure to hit the bull's eye is never the fault of the target. To improve your aim, improve yourself.
Gilbert Arland

The central adventure in life: the search for your ultimate purpose.
Lorna Catford and Michael Ray

Resolve to be thyself: and know, that he who finds himself, loses his misery.
Matthew Arnold

Don't limit yourself. Many people limit themselves to what they think they can do. You can go as far as your mind lets you. What you believe you can achieve.
Mary Kay Ash

Let every man be respected as an individual and no man idolised.
Albert Einstein

Low self-esteem is like driving through life with your hand-brake on.
Maxwell Maltz

No one can make you feel inferior without your permission.
Eleanor Roosevelt

They are the weakest, however strong, who have no faith in themselves or their own power.
Christian Bovee

BE YOUR OWN SELF-ESTEEM COACH

To establish true self-esteem we must concentrate on our successes and forget about the failures and the negatives in our lives.
Denis Waitley

Whatever good things we build end up building us.
Jim Rohn

I was not looking for my dreams to interpret my life, but rather for my life to interpret my dreams.
Susan Sontag

If one advances confidently in the direction of his dreams…he will meet with a success unexpected in common hours.
Henry David Thoreau

I don't know the key to success. But the key to failure is trying to please everyone else.
Bill Cosby

Reflect upon your present blessings of which every man has plenty, not upon your past misfortunes of which all men have some.
Charles Dickens

The best and most beautiful things in the world cannot be seen or even touched. They must be felt in the human heart.
Helen Keller

The positive thinker sees the invisible, feels the intangible and achieves the impossible.
Anon

It is not a disaster to capture your ideals, but it is a disaster to have no ideals to capture.
Benjamin Mays

If there is no enemy within, the enemy outside can do you no harm.
African Proverb

The man who goes alone can start today; but he who travels with another must wait until the other is ready.
Henry David Thoreau

APPENDIX ONE: SELF-ESTEEM QUOTATIONS

There's this guy who walks down the street one day and falls straight into a hole. And the next day he walks down the same street and tries to jump over it, but falls in again. Then on the third day he approaches the hole really slowly, and tries to walk around the edge, but still falls in. The day after he takes a different street. You know what I mean? Sometimes it takes a little while to learn how to deal with the world.
Liza Minnelli

Your friend is the person who knows all about you and still likes you.
Elbert Hubbard

When to give up? Never, never, never.
Winston Churchill

Your vision will become clear only when you look into your heart… Who looks outside dreams. Who looks inside awakens.
Carl Jung

There is a time in the life of every problem when it is big enough to see yet small enough to solve.
Mike Leavitt

The harder you prepare, the luckier you get.
Doug Collins

Accept that some days you're the pigeon and some days you are the statue.
Roger C Anderson

In the world to come I shall not be asked, 'Why were you not Moses?' I should be asked, 'Why were you not Zusya?'
Rabbi Zusya

The greatest discovery of my generation is that human beings can alter their lives by altering their attitudes of mind.
William James

Keep away from people who belittle your ambitions. Small people always do that, but the really great make you feel that you, too, can become great.
Mark Twain

BE YOUR OWN SELF-ESTEEM COACH

To touch the soul of another human being is to walk on holy ground.
Stephen R Covey

Oh the worst of all tragedies is not to die young, but to live until I am seventy-five and yet not ever truly have lived.
Martin Luther King Junior

The confidence which we have in ourselves gives birth to much of that which we have in others.
François de la Rochefoucald

Since ancient times, the wise ones have said that our greatest quest in life is self-knowledge.
Gill Edwards

Three things in human life are important: the first is to be kind. The second is to be kind. And the third is to be kind.
Henry James

Though no one can go back and make a brand new start, anyone can start from now and make a brand new ending.
Anon

You have not lived a perfect day, even though you have earned your money, unless you have done something for someone who will never be able to repay you.
Ruth Smeltzer

When you give of yourself, you receive more than you give.
Antoine de Saint-Exupéry

A thousand words will not leave so deep an impression as one deed.
Henrik Ibsen

The hero therefore, is the man or woman who has been able to battle past his personal and local historical limitations.
Joseph Campbell

The unexamined life is not worth living.
Plato

APPENDIX ONE: SELF-ESTEEM QUOTATIONS

Come to the edge, he said.
They said, We are afraid.
Come to the edge, he said.
They came.
He pushed them ... And they flew.
Guillame Apollinaire

If winter comes, can spring be far behind?
Percy Bysshe Shelley

All men's miseries derive from not being able to sit quiet in a room alone.
Blaise Pascal

People don't care about how much you know, until they know how much you care.
John Hanley

The deepest principle in human nature is the craving to be appreciated.
William James

There are two things people want more than sex and money—that's praise and recognition.
Mary Kay Ash

The goal of the recovery process is not to become normal ... The goal is to become the unique, awesome, never to be repeated human being that we are called to be.
Patricia Deegan

You always miss 100% of the shots that you don't take.
Wayne Gretzky

Peace comes within the souls of men when they realise their oneness with the universe.
Black Elk

May I take this opportunity to wish you continued success in your career and also in your life, which is undeniably far more important.
Phil Barker

In the depths of winter, I finally learned that there was within me an invincible summer.
Albert Camus

BE YOUR OWN SELF-ESTEEM COACH

Believe that life is worth living and your belief will help create the fact.
William James

Make a memory with your children,
Spend some time to show you care.
Toys and trinkets can't replace those
Precious moments that you share.
Elaine Hardt

The important thing is this: to be able at any moment to sacrifice what we are for what we could become.
Charles du Bois

Commit random acts of kindness, perform senseless acts of beauty.
Anon

Where there is great love there are always miracles.
Willa Cather

Ordinary men hate solitude,
But the master makes use of it,
Embracing his wholeness, realising
He is one with the whole universe.
Lao-tzu

The heights by great men reached and kept were not attained by sudden flight, but they, while their companions slept, were toiling upward in the night.
Longfellow

Life is mostly froth and bubble, two things stand like stone, kindness in another's troubles, courage in your own.
Adam Lindsey Gordon

A happy person is not a person in a certain set of circumstances, but rather a person with a certain set of attitudes.
Hugh Downs

Twenty years from now you will be more disappointed by the things that you didn't do that by the ones you did do. So throw off your bowlines. Sail away from the safe harbour. Catch the trade winds in your sails. Explore. Dream. Discover.
Mark Twain

APPENDIX ONE: SELF-ESTEEM QUOTATIONS

The more faithfully you listen to the voice within you, the better you hear what is sounding outside of you.
Dag Hammarskjöld

Life's most urgent question is: what are you doing for others?
Martin Luther King Junior

For everything you have missed, you have gained something else.
Ralph Waldo Emerson

Start by doing what's necessary, then what's possible and suddenly you are doing the impossible.
StFrancis of Assisi

Example is not the only thing in influencing others. It is the only thing.
Albert Schweitzer

Nothing in the world can take the place of persistence. Talent will not; nothing in the world is more common that unsuccessful men with talent. Genius will not; unrewarded genius is a proverb. Education will not; the world is full of educated derelicts. Persistence and determination are omnipotent.
Calvin Coolidge

You can do more for your own health and well-being than any doctor, any hospital, any drug, and exotic medical advice.
US Surgeon General's Report, 1979

Spread love wherever you go ... first of all in your own house. Give love to your children, to your wife or husband, to a next door neighbour…let no one ever come to you without leaving better and happier. Be the living expression of God's kindness; kindness in your face, kindness in your eyes, kindness in your smile, kindness in your warm greeting.
Mother Teresa

When the pupil is ready, the teacher will appear.
Anon

APPENDIX TWO

INSPIRATIONAL PROSE AND POETRY

We are challenged on every hand to work untiringly to achieve excellence in our lifework. Not all men are called to specialised or professional jobs: even fewer rise to the heights of genius in the arts and sciences; many are called to be labourers in factories, fields and streets. But no work is insignificant. All labour that uplifts humanity has dignity and importance and should be undertaken with painstaking excellence. If a man is called to be a streetsweeper, he should sweep even as Michelangelo painted, or Beethoven composed music, or Shakespeare wrote poetry. He should sweep streets so well that all the host of heaven and earth will pause to say, 'Here lived a great street sweeper who did his job well.'
Martin Luther King Junior

The Mullah to a harlot said:
'When you entice men to your bed,
Do you not in your heart repine
To live a slave to lust and wine?'
But she upon his words broke in:
'I am adept in every sin;
'Tis my career-can you profess
To follow yours with like success.'
Omar Khayyam

If
If you think you are beaten, you are.
If you think you dare not, you don't.
If you'd like to win, but think you can't
It's almost certain you won't.

BE YOUR OWN SELF-ESTEEM COACH

If you think you'll lose, you've lost.
For out of the world we find
Success begins with a fellow's will-
It's all in the state of mind.
If you think you're outclassed, you are.
You've got to think high to rise.
You've got to be sure of yourself before
You can ever win a prize.
Life's battles don't always go
To the stronger or faster person.
But sooner or later the person who wins
Is the one who Thinks they can.
Anon

The Human Body at peace with itself,
Is more precious than the rarest gem.
Cherish your body, it is yours one time only.
The human form is won with difficulty,
It is easy to lose.
All worldly things are brief,
Like lightning in the sky;
This life you must know as the tiny
Splash of a raindrop;
A thing of beauty that disappears
Even as it comes into being.
Therefore set your goal.
Make use of every day and night to achieve it.
Anon

To laugh is to risk appearing the fool.
To weep is to risk appearing sentimental.
To reach out for another is to risk involvement.
To expose feelings is to risk expressing one's true self.
To place your ideas, your dreams, before the crowd is to risk loss.
To love is to risk not being loved in return.
To live is to risk dying.
To hope is to risk despair.
To try at all is to risk failure.
But risk we must, because the greatest hazard in life is to risk

APPENDIX TWO: INSPIRATIONAL PROSE AND POETRY

nothing.
The man, the woman, who risks nothing, does nothing, has nothing, is nothing.
Anon

Success
To laugh often and much.
To win the respect of intelligent people
And affection of children;
To earn the appreciation of honest critics
And endure the betrayals of false friends;
To appreciate beauty, to find the best in others;
To leave the world a bit better, whether by a healthy child,
A garden patch or a redeemed social condition;
To know even one life has breathed easier because you have lived.
This is to have succeeded.
Ralph Waldo Emerson

A Creed to Live by
Don't undermine your worth by comparing yourself with others.
It is because we are different that each of us is special.
Don't set your goals by what other people deem important.
Only you know what is best for you.
Don't take for granted the things closest to your heart.
Cling to them as you would your life, for without them life is meaningless.
Don't let your life slip through your fingers
By living in the past or for the future.
By living your life one day at a time
You live all the days of your life.
Don't give up when you still have something to give.
Nothing is really over until the moment you stop trying.
Don't be afraid to admit that you are less than perfect.
It is this fragile thread that binds us to each other.
Don't be afraid to encounter risks.
It is by taking chances that we learn to be brave.
Don't shut love out of your life, by saying it's impossible to find.
The quickest way to receive love is to give love,
The fastest way to lose love is to hold it too tightly,

BE YOUR OWN SELF-ESTEEM COACH

And the best way to keep love is to give it wings.
Don't dismiss your dreams.
To be without dreams is to be without hope,
To be without hope is to be without purpose.
Don't run through life so fast that you forget
Not only where you've been, but also where you're going.
Life is not a race, but a journey to be savoured
Each step of the way.
Anon

Life is
A mystery, unfold it.
A journey, walk it.
Painful, endure it.
Beautiful, see it.
A joke, laugh at it.
A song. Sing it.
A flower, smell it.
Wonderful, enjoy it.
A candle, light it.
Precious, don't waste it.
A gift, open it. Love, give it.
Unlimited, go for it.
Light, shine on it.
I AM ALL THAT LIFE IS.
Jewel Diamond Taylor

10 Commandments for a Happy Life
Today, I will be grateful for all I have. I will not be envious of others who seem to have more material goods than I have.

Today, I will not get angry or concern myself with unimportant trifles.

Today, I will not let the wrong doings of others cause me to do wrong.
Today, I will not be proud and look down on others.

Today, I will not criticise or find fault.

Today, I will do a good thing for someone else, it will not be

APPENDIX TWO: INSPIRATIONAL PROSE AND POETRY

something for which I expect something in return.

Today, I will keep busy and work hard as long as I am in good health,. I will not be lazy or idle, though I will find a quiet hour for myself.

Today, I will be the best I can be, I will be sincere in my thoughts and generous in my relations with others.

Today, I will live for today because yesterday has gone and tomorrow may never come.

Today, I will truly try to like all those with whom I come into contact with.

Anon

BE YOUR OWN SELF-ESTEEM COACH

APPENDIX THREE

AFFIRMATIONS

(This is an additional set of affirmations that I have adapted from the Internet (see: http://www.mjbovo.com/Affirmations.htm). Personally, I am happier with the Canfield and Branden methods, but you need to see which approach is best for you).

Affirmations are statements of acceptance ... They are powerful and positive thoughts and statements ... To do positive affirmations, you need to eliminate the negativity around you. You must first believe that YOU CAN manifest your destiny. It must be a positive, powerful belief not just 'maybe I'll try and see if this works.'

Before you begin

Decide what area of your life you want to work on and then decide what you want. There are several important points to know about affirmations:

- *Use the present or past tense.* Do not use the future tense. You want your mind to know it has already happened.

- *Be positive.* Use the most positive terms you can. Never use negatives in affirmations.

- *Write them.* As you are learning to do affirmations, write them down so you will remember exactly what you want to say. Keep them short and very specific. Personalise them with your name.

- *Believe.* Always believe that what you are saying is happening. The more you believe, the stronger the affirmation.

- *Repetition.* Being repetitive and persistent helps to set them in your head and in your unconscious being.

- *Time.* Always have a specific time set aside each day for your meditations, affirmations and visualisations. This will help set a pattern for you so you will do them daily.

Affirmations for Daily Living

- I am at peace with the universe.

- I love and accept myself.

- I am unique and loving, loved and free.

- I am safe and always feel protected.

- I acknowledge all of my feelings because I am in touch with my feelings.

- I am surrounded with loving, caring people in my life.

- I am loving and accepting of others and this creates lasting friendships for me.

- I trust my inner being to lead me in the right path.

- I do all I can every day to make a loving environment for all those around me, including myself.

- My inner vision is always clear and focussed.

APPENDIX THREE: AFFIRMATIONS

Affirmations for Health

- I have the power to control my health.
- I am in control of my health and wellness.
- I have abundant energy, vitality and well-being.
- I am healthy in all aspects of my being.
- I do not fear being unhealthy because I know I can control my own body.
- I am always able to maintain my ideal weight.
- I am filled with energy to do all the daily activities in my life.
- My mind is at rest.
- I love and care for my body and it cares for me.

Affirmations for Abundance

- I am a success in all that I do.
- Everything I touch returns riches to me.
- I am always productive.
- My work is always recognised positively
- I respect my abilities and always work to my full potential.
- I am constantly adding to my income.
- I always spend money wisely.
- I always have enough money for all that I need.
- I am rewarded for all the work that I do.

Affirmations for Peace and Harmony in your Life

- I am at peace with myself.
- I am always at harmony with the universe.
- I am peace with all those around me.
- I have provided a harmonious place for myself and those I love.
- The more honest I am with those around me, the more love is returned to me.
- I express anger in appropriate ways so that peace and harmony are balanced at all times.

Affirmations for my Spirituality

- I am free to be myself.
- I am a forgiving and loving person.
- I am responsible for my own spiritual growth.
- My strength comes from forgiveness of those who hurt me.
- I am worthy of love.
- The more I love, the more that love is returned to me.
- Love is eternal and ever-lasting.
- I am responsible for my life and always maintain the power I need to be positive and have joy.